THE **CHRISTIAN** IN THE CHINESE CULTURE

About the author
Boon-Sing Poh was born in Malaysia in 1954. Brought up in a pagan background, he was saved by God's grace through faith in Jesus Christ while studying in the United Kingdom. He returned to Malaysia to become a lecturer in a university for six years, founded the first Reformed Baptist Church in the country in 1983, and was imprisoned for his faith from 1987 to 1988 for a period of 325 days. He is the pastor of Damansara Reformed Baptist Church (DRBC) in Kuala Lumpur, a contented husband, a thankful father of four sons, and a happy grandfather. He earned the PhD degree in Electronics Engineering from the University of Liverpool, UK, the Diploma in Religious Study from Cambridge University, UK, and the PhD degree in Theology from North-West University, SA.

THE **CHRISTIAN** IN THE **CHINESE CULTURE**

BOON-SING POH

Published by
Good News Enterprise

THE CHRISTIAN IN THE CHINESE CULTURE

ISBN: 978-983-9180-40-4

First published: 1986
Second edition: 1989
Third edition: April 2020
This imprint: February 2024

Published by:

GOOD NEWS ENTERPRISE, 52 Jalan SS 21/2,
Damansara Utama, 47400 Petaling Jaya, Malaysia.
www.rbcm.net; www.ghmag.net

Printed by:
Kindle Direct Publishing, an Amazon company, United States of America.
Limited copies printed by James Aries Printing Sdn. Bhd., 40 Jalan TPK 2/5, Taman Perindustrian Kinrara, 47100 Petaling Jaya, Malaysia.
Typeset by the author using TeXworks, the memoir class.

This book is dedicated to

Belvidere Road Church (1976-1981)

Liverpool, U.K.

from where I learned so much.

Contents

ACKNOWLEDGEMENT

The author would like to thank the following people:

1 His parents (father now deceased), mother-in-law, and sister for helpful discussions on the Chinese festivals. His sister, Boon Lian, also supplied the Chinese characters and checked up many of the dates in this book.

2 Pastor Charles M. C. Cheung of Sydney, Australia, for his helpful comments and constructive criticism.

3 His wife, Good Cam, for typing the many drafts of the manuscript (before the days of the desktop and laptop computers).

4 Members of the Sri Serdang Church (1983-1991) for their fellowship and encouragement in the faith. Three of them – Miranda Yeoh, Lyn Fiona, and Debra Sim – were directly involved in preparing this book for publication (of the first edition).

5 Dr. Samuel E. Boyle (1905-2002) of Shawnee, USA, former missionary to Southern China and Japan, for his encouragement to get this book published – and this despite his physical infirmities.

Bible quotations in this book are taken from the New King James Version except where otherwise stated. The present author alone is to be held responsible for the contents of this book.

PREFACE TO THIS EDITION

This book has been out of print for a long time. Enquiries for the book have come in from various parts of the world through the years. One such that came in recently says,

> In the Lord's goodness a number of Chinese families have come into our meetings. We were wondering whether your book "The Christian in the Chinese Culture" is available.

Another reader says, among other things,

> Many years ago I read with much profit your book, "The Christian in the Chinese Culture". My Hindu family have never accepted that I have become a Christian. In order to avoid family intrusion and interference into our marriage we have moved away. Every time I have been to see them, they harangued me that I no longer love them. Seeing them steeped in Hinduism, I come away so depressed that it takes me six months to recover, each time. This is particularly hard for my wife. As a pastor converted from Chinese culture which is similar to Hinduism, what Biblical counsel would you offer me?

The busyness and trials of ministry have prevented a republication of the book until now. The book was originally written when the desktop computer was beginning to make its appearance. The laptop computer was still unheard of. With the advent of the internet, there was a personal struggle over whether the book should be re-written, to include more supportive references. However, upon reflection, and in consideration of enquiries such as the above, it was decided that the original objective of helping others should hold sway. Minimal touch-up of the material has been made, and an additional chapter entitled "Chinese Arts and Philosophy" has been included. This chapter arose from talks given at a Missions Conference some years after the publication of the book. Its style, therefore, differs from that rest of the book. Its relevance to the subject at hand, however, is obvious. An appendix, entitled "The Romance of the Three Kingdoms", which was first published in the Gospel Highway magazine in 1996, is also included. Another Appendix, entitled "China and the Chinese Diaspora", published in GRACE Magazine, November 2002 is included as well.

The new generation of mainland Chinese will not be familiar with the raw paganism covered in this book. They are more influenced by materialism, science, and technology. However, it will be difficult for them to emotionally sever themselves from their historical root which includes the paganism still seen in Hong Kong, in Taiwan, and among the Chinese of the diaspora. Songs such as "Descendants of the Dragon" (龙的传人) and "My Chinese Heart" (我的中国心) continue to stir the inner psyche of the Chinese worldwide. Our objective of being of help to others applies to them as well. This edition of the book uses simplified Chinese and the Pingyin system of transliterating the Chinese characters.

May the triune God use this book to edify a new generation of His people, and save many souls.

Boon-Sing Poh,
Kuala Lumpur, April 2020.

PREFACE

Many are the Christians who have been converted from a background of the Chinese Religion. Being first-generation Christians, they face many problems from their unconverted families. As Christians, they have to live in a way that is consistent with their faith. As Chinese, they still have to live within the Chinese culture. Help from Christian quarters concerning how to live the Christian life in the Chinese family is hard to come by. The little advice given by well-meaning, but ill-informed, Christian friends often prove to be impractical. Who can understand the difficulties, the struggles and the temptations that come the way of the Chinese Christians?

Having been brought up in a family that practises the Chinese Religion, I sense keenly the responsibility to help others who may be facing such difficulties. In putting these pages to print, I am in no way claiming to have *the* answer to every problem. Also, constant reference is made to the "average" Chinese or the "average" Christian. By "average" I do not mean someone who is average in intelligence or attainment but rather someone whose values and principles are in common with the majority of modern-day Chinese or Christians. While recognising that the situation is different in each family, it is hoped that this book will be of help to other Chinese Christians. The Christian who is from a different religious background in which idol worship is practised may find this book helpful too.

The original draft of this book was ready in 1982. By the providence of God, it was not published. As the years passed by, I have had opportunity to travel and interact with believers in various parts of Malaysia. The conviction grew stronger and stronger in me that there is a need for this book to be published. The original draft was therefore re-edited into its present form.

The substance of this book has been presented in a series of studies in our church. Our people have found it helpful. The questions used in that series of studies are now gathered together at the end of this book. It is hoped that, in this way, the book may be used as a manual for group study. My suggestion is that the group leader presents the substance of a chapter, summarising wherever necessary, and then uses the questions for group discussion. Alternatively, every member in the group may read a chapter in advance so that when the group meets, there is more time for discussion after the leader has summarised the chapter.

Wherever necessary, footnotes are included in the relevant pages. Other notes and references to books are gathered together at the end of this book in order not to interrupt the flow of the reading. Longer notes are included in the Appendices.

It is my prayer that God will use this book to advance His kingdom on earth and build up His church, causing the name of the Lord Jesus Christ to be uplifted and magnified.

Boon-Sing Poh, 1986

One

THE CHINESE RELIGION (Eccl. 1:1-18)

Strange as it might sound, we find it necessary to invent a name, *the Chinese Religion*, to describe the religious beliefs and practices of the Chinese people. Having coined this name, we need to explain what is meant by it. This is because the new generation of overseas Chinese have only a vague idea of the religious beliefs that have been handed down in their families.

There is a strong element of animism in the religious life of the Chinese. That is why shrines are built beside big trees and ant-hills to worship the spirits that are supposed to be dwelling in them. However, these beliefs and practices fit into the overall religious scheme that was brought out from China by the early overseas Chinese. We shall, therefore, concentrate on the main influences that mould what we call *the Chinese Religion*.

1.1   What Is The Chinese Religion?

The Chinese Religion is a mixture of Confucianism, Daoism and Buddhism. Because of this, the average Chinese is often at a loss for an answer when asked what is his religion. He sometimes answers that it is Chinese Buddhism; at other times he would say it is Daoism; and at yet other times it is Ancestral Worship. For our purpose here, we shall call it *the Chinese Religion*.

Confucianism has contributed to the moral-intellectual aspect of the Chinese Religion while Daoism has given to it its mystical content. Buddhism has contributed to the philosophical-metaphysical content of the Chinese Religion. It came from India to China in the first century AD, and was quickly assimilated by the Chinese (Lee, S. M., 1983).

The Chinese Religion has diffused into nearly all areas of the Chinese life so that it is hard to find an area in which we can say is totally free from any element of the religion. At a birth, the year is noted since it corresponds to one of the twelve animals of the Chinese zodiac. At a wedding, the bride and groom pray to the family altar. At a funeral, monks are invited to conduct an elaborate ceremony. When learning *Gongfu* (known outside China as *Kung-fu*, the Chinese arts of self-defence), the students pray to the various Chinese gods. When buying a house or siting a grave, the advice of knowledgeable friends or mediums is sought to determine whether the location or *Fengshui* (风水) is right. When sending a son or daughter overseas for further studies, charms (which often consist of yellow strips of paper with red markings on them) are obtained from mediums and given to him/her for protection. When buying four-digit lotteries, the family altar is prayed to and the help of mediums is sought for good-luck. Even the initiation ceremonies of secret societies are full of religious rites.

It is possible to argue theoretically that culture and religion are different, though intertwined. Culture covers all aspects of our life whereas religion covers only the spiritual side. In other words, religion is just one aspect of culture, which is all-embracing. In practice, however, the Chinese Religion has diffused into nearly all aspects of the Chinese life so much so that to talk about Chinese culture, one cannot escape talking about the Chinese Religion as well.

The Influence Of Confucianism
Ancestral worship is often spoken of as though it is the religion of the Chinese. It is, in fact, only one aspect of the Chinese Religion. Ancestral worship, which appears linked to spirit-worship, is nothing more than an act of filial piety which was taught by Confucius, or Kong Zi (孔子) in Chinese. To honour one's parents means not only obedience to them when they are living but also worshipping them when they are dead.

Confucius was not just a philosopher and a moral teacher, but also a political theorist. He saw that the family unit is the key to a successful and united nation. The individual as a member of a family is, thus, the logical place to begin consideration for any statesman. The individual's body is regarded as the sacred inheritance from the parents. The Five Cardinal Virtues as taught by Confucius are: to live a principled life, to be faithful to one's friends, to be loyal to the state, to be honest in official duty, and to be courageous on the battle field. Failure in any one of these five duties will disgrace one's parents (Lee, S. M., 1983; E. B. 4:1108).

In the past, the ideal of Chinese parents was to train up their children to be good scholars as well as good fighters. The pen and the sword were to go hand in hand. This is expressed as *wen wu shuang quan* (文武双全), which is equivalent to "Brains and brawn". (The Chinese places brains first.) For this reason, a picture of Guan Yu (关羽) (or Guan Gong, 关公), the famous Chinese general, would depict him reading a book, while a picture of Confucius, the scholar, would depict him carrying a sword on his waist. The exploits of Guan Yu and his two companions Zhang Fei (张飞) and Liu Bei (刘备) are described in the Chinese classic "San Guo Yan Yi" (三国演义) written by one Luo Guanzhong (罗贯中) during the transition period between the Yuan (1279-1368) and the Ming (1368-1644) dynasties. The book is known in the West as "Romance of the Three Kingdoms". The three characters in the book have been raised to the position of the deities and are worshipped in many Chinese homes today.

It should be noted that many such deities were only men of the past, great though they might have been. Also, veneration of the deceased is the outcome of the teaching of Confucius (551-479 BC) who was only a man, clever though he might have been.

The Influence Of Buddhism

Buddhism was brought to China from India in the first century AD. Buddhism as a religion captured the Chinese mind to a much greater extent than is commonly recognised. Its doctrine of the transmigration of the soul can be said to be complementary to Confucianism. Confucianism has not much to say about life after death nor about the spiritual realm. Buddhism gives the Chinese an intelligent scheme of what happens to the soul after death. It is taught that the soul goes to the spirit-world and, with time, would be given the physical body of a man or an animal through rebirth, depending on how well the person had lived in his previous earthly life. This process of reincarnation would be repeated according to the Law of Karma and, for practical purposes, appears infinite. Only the Buddhist teachings on meditation and abstention from worldly desires can bring it to an absolute end, when the deathless state of enlightenment, or *nirvana*, is reached (EB, 3:422).

The average Chinese is pragmatic and does not concern himself with the details of the Law of Karma. The state of *nirvana* is vaguely associated with the heaven of Daoism, and failure to attain *nirvana* with hell. While living, he tries to live a virtuous life. When there is a death in the family, he mourns and obediently carries out the necessary rituals. Paper models of money, a house, a car and servants are burnt so that the soul of the deceased may have access to these items in his travel through the spirit-world. The clothing of the deceased is often burned because it is not as valuable an item as a real house or a real car. Moreover, no one in the family would want to wear the clothes left by the deceased.

Buddhism as a philosophy exerted a great scholastic influence on the Chinese mind and inspired many Chinese writings. As a result, much of the classical Chinese literature shows Buddhist influence in it. Stories about Guan Yin (观音) or the Goddess of Mercy, the monk Tang Zang (唐僧), the Monkey King (孙悟空), Pigsy (猪八戒), and Sandy (沙悟净) are well-known to the Chinese. These stories are found in the Chinese classic "Xi You Ji" (西游记), or "Journey To The West", written by Wu Chen'en (吴承恩) during the Ming Dynasty (1368-1644). The Goddess of Mercy is worshipped in many Chinese homes today. Her origin has been traced to Avalokitesvara of Buddhism, a male figure who apparently merged with Chinese myths of goddesses and with time became increasingly conceived as a female figure (EB, 3:397).

One such myths tells of a good-hearted princess, Miao Li (妙丽), who sacrificed her eyes and hands in order that these might be mixed with a herbal brew to cure her tyrannical father of a fatal disease. After a period of fasting, Miao Li's sight and hands were restored and she was elevated to become Guan Yin, the Goddess of Mercy, and was worshipped by her repentant father.

Another Chinese classic is "Feng Shen Bang" (封神榜), or "Investiture Of The Gods", written by Xu Zhonglin (许仲琳) during the Ming Dynasty. A well-known mythical character in it is Ne Zha (哪吒). The story goes that Ne Zha, who did not get on well with his father, renounced his family by cutting out the flesh from his own body in order to return it to them. His soul travelled to his *Gongfu* master who remade a physical body for him using lotus leaves. The idol of Ne Zha is easily recognised in any Chinese temple. It shows him carrying a spear in one hand and a large ring in the other, and under each of his feet is a ring of fire on which he travels.

Another mythical figure from this latter classic who has been deified by the Chinese is Ji Gong (济公). He is a smiling monk who flies about on a straw fan and wears a saddle-shaped hat that, when thrown, can magically become so big as to trap an enemy under it. Included in his many exploits is his travel to hell, from which he returned to be the expert teacher on what hell is like. Ji Gong is worshipped in many Chinese temple today.

Yet another Chinese god who has his origin in this classic is the Dragon-god-of-the-sea (海龙王). He has the body of a human being and the head of a dragon, just as the Monkey King and Pigsy have bodies of human beings and heads of a monkey and a pig, respectively. The different categories of dragons, according to Chinese mythology, were the heavenly, the earthly, the treasure guarding, the spiritual, and the imperial (Kong, B. and Ho, E. H., 1973). The dragon was probably a sea-serpent originally. It became the symbol of the male principle. Together with the phoenix, which represents the female principle, they are often shown on invitation cards to a Chinese wedding. The dragon had been the symbol of Chinese royalty, and had been widely used by the Chinese, long before the Dragon-god-of-the-sea was invented. This has to be so because monkeys and pigs were already in existence before the Monkey King and Pigsy were invented. The Dragon-god-of-the-sea is worshipped by many fishermen today.

It can be seen that many deities worshipped by the Chinese are really legendary or mythical[1] figures created by Chinese scholars who were only human beings. Also, many religious rituals arose from Buddhism, the religion founded by Buddha (563-483 BC) who was only a man, pious though he might have been.

---

[1] Legends are traditional stories, told as a matter of history, about particular persons or places, the details of which are of doubtful truth. Myths are accounts about gods or superhuman beings and their extraordinary exploits which are imaginary, fictitious or invented. The stories contained in San Guo Yan Yi are basically legends, while those contained in Xi You Ji and Feng Shen Bang are basically myths.

The Influence Of Daoism

Lao Zi (老子, 604-531 BC) is often accredited to be the founder of Daoism and author of the "Dao De Jing" ("Classic of the Way of Integrity"). However, a philosophical cosmology already existed in an elementary form long before his time. Fuxi (伏牺), the first of China's mythical emperors who was supposed to have lived in the 29th century BC, is said to have invented the Bagua (八卦), the famous Eight Trigrams used for divination (EB, Micropaedia IV: 345). Fuxi is regarded as a mythical and divine ruler with the body of a snake who gave humanity the skills of animal husbandry, fishing with nets, and hunting with iron weapons. The Dao De Jing (道德经) must not be confused with another book called the Yi Jing (易经), another ancient classic of Daoism. The Yi Jing is a book of divination which applies the Yin-Yang (阴阳) principle and the Bagua concept to life.

Daoism, like Confucianism, aimed at the attainment of peace and contentment in an ordered society. Confucius approached the objective from the upper ruling class of scholars while Lao Zi approached it from below (Lee, S. M., 1983). Lao Zi's doctrine of *wu wei* (无为) often translated as "inaction" or "effortlessness", has been adopted by Chinese Buddhism. During the Han Dynasty (206 BC-220 AD), Confucianism, Daoism and Buddhism were merged into a common philosophy that undergirds the Chinese Religion.

Daoism as a religion developed occultism, which includes such practices as mediumship, astrology, fortune-telling and communication with the dead. It lends to the Chinese Religion a mystical aura in which superstitious beliefs develop and thrive. From such an atmosphere has arisen the grotesque and fanciful ideas of ghosts, heaven and hell. Ghosts are often depicted as beings in human forms with long dishevelled hair and tongues sticking out a foot or more, and they glide about silently with the feet not touching the ground. Heaven is somewhere in the skies where immortal fairies, both male and female, float about on clouds with the look of contentment on their faces. The fairies form an hierarchy in which Buddha is the highest and most powerful of them all. Hell is a place of torment and fire somewhere deep in the earth where long-tongued ghosts dwell.

Anyone who observes the occult practices of the Chinese Religion today would be perplexed by the unusual things that the mediums are capable of doing. When consulted by devotees, a medium would speak in an unintelligible tongue that needs to be interpreted by someone else. A medium in a trance is able to do such seemingly impossible feats as walking bare-footed on hot burning embers without harming himself, revealing secrets, and curing diseases.

The Chinese not only acknowledge readily that spiritist forces are at work in the world but also classify the spirits into good and wicked ones. What is not often recognised is that the spirits are all the accomplices of the devil, the father of all lies, whether they pose as good or wicked ones. (See also Appendix 1.)

Again, we should note that Lao Zi (604-531 BC.), the founder of Daoism, was only a man, however great a philosopher he might have been. We note also that the many superstitious beliefs of the Chinese flow from the imagination of men, and the devil easily takes advantage of an atmosphere of mysticism to hold captive the minds of people.

1.2 The Chinese Religion Unmasked

The art of Bian Lian (变脸) or "Face-Changing", which originated from the Sichuan opera, is today widely performed during Chinese cultural shows. It is entertaining, and shocking, to see the one performer changing his face in an instant, a number of times, to convey different moods. The different faces of the Chinese Religion may amuse or scare the onlooker. On the natural dimension, the Chinese Religion is nothing more than humanism. Humanism is a system of thought or teaching that concerns itself, not with divine, but with human interests. Humanism puts man as the centre of its greatest concern. It exalts man instead of God. As a philosophy, it makes man the measure of all things.

The humanism in the Chinese shows itself in his unquestioning acceptance of all the religious rituals and traditional beliefs that have been handed down. The Chinese would continue to burn joss-sticks and offer fruits and cakes to the family altar at home for as long as it makes him feel good and it harms no one. The two prime motives that make him pray to the various gods are for the gods to grant him material prosperity and protection from calamities in his family. He tolerates all other religions and is willing to worship their gods as well if only they can fulfil his desires for prosperity and freedom from calamities. He appeals only for others not to interfere with, or criticise, his form of worship. All religions are the same to him in that they lead to the same end, which is the good of mankind.

To be sure, the Chinese are not the only people who are humanists. Humanism is the hallmark of modern men throughout the world today. Men are either non-theistic humanists or they believe and practise a theistic humanism in which the gods of their religions are given attributes conjured up by the human mind. Among the latter are modern-day liberal Christian theologians who trim down the God of the Bible to the manageable size of their puny minds. Our analysis of the Chinese Religion has shown that the religion is man-created and man-centred. It is a form of theistic humanism.

From the spiritual perspective, however, we must understand that the devil may appear in different guises to deceive people (cf. 2 Cor. 11:14). His primary aim is to capture the mind and win the allegiance of the person to himself. He deceives and manipulates to achieve his own ends. He has a host of fallen angels working for him. We are engaged in a spiritual warfare (Eph. 6:12). This aspect of the Chinese Religion will become clear by and by.

Questions

1 Confucius taught people to honour their parents. How does this teaching compare with, and differ from, the Bible's teaching? (See Ex. 20:12; Eph. 6:1-2).

2 What would you say to a couple who desires to train up their children Confucian-style, so that they are good with the pen and the sword (i.e. to be good at studies and in the martial arts)?

3 Are the Chinese the only people who are humanists? Can we consider the modern-day liberal Christian theologians as humanist? Why?

4 Would you object to Christian children reading stories from the Chinese classics like "San Guo Yan Yi", "Xi You Ji" and "Feng Shen Bang"? Why?

References

1 Encyclopaedia Britannica.

2 Encyclopaedia Britannica, Micropaedia.

3 Kong, Bucksom, and Ho, Eugene H., 1973. Hung Gar Kung-fu. Starnd Book Co., Malaysia.

4 Lee, Siow Mong, 1983. Chinese Culture And Religion. Wisdom Series No. 11. Buddhist Missionary Society, Kuala Lumpur.

Two

Chinese Arts And Philosophy (Eccl. 3:1-22)

> [I]t is clear that the *possessio*, the taking possession of the entire life, is in practice far from simple. Nothing is neutral in life; dangers are at every hand. A strong and real Christian faith is needed to break a path through these forests of difficulties without being scratched. If young churches live close to Christ, attentively listen to the Scriptures, and allow themselves to be led by them, here also we may hope for fresh new dynamics... It is more and more clear, however, that the pioneer work must here be done by the sons and daughters of the young churches (Bavinck, 1961: 190).

I write this as a son of such a young church. I am a first-generation Christian, converted from a pagan Chinese culture, and now ministers in a pagan culture in which the main eastern religions hold sway. I am conscious that mine is only *a* Christian perspective, not *the* Christian perspective, to the subject at hand.

Our interest here is not with the so-called "fine arts", namely painting, dance, music, and poetry. Rather, our concern is with those branches of studies and skills that have developed within the Chinese culture, including the martial arts, *Qigong*, medical practice, and *Fengshui*. Underlying these arts is the system of thought which encompasses the principles of "Yin and Yang", "the Five Elements" and "Bagua". These principles are distinct but inter-related. They have been applied separately, or in conjunction with one another. We begin, therefore, with a consideration of these principles, under the heading of Chinese Philosophy.[1]

2.1 Chinese Philosophy

The Yin-Yang principle
Ancient Chinese philosophers called the void and boundless state which prevailed before the world was created *wuji*, or "ultimate nothingness". From this state of *wuji* was formed the universe. *Wuji* may be thought of as a condition as well as a thing. It had form, yet was unformed. It had shape, yet without shape. This phenomenon of "nothingness" was the source of movement and stillness.

The state of *wuji* was regarded as being made up of the *yin* element. Within the *yin* was the germ of the *yang* element. When the *yang* element began to manifest itself, the state of *wuji* or nothingness no longer existed. At that point, the state of *taiji* began. *Taiji* may be translated "the great ultimate" or "the grand terminus". *Yin* and *yang* began to interact with one another in a complementary way. Although they are opposite in nature, there is a harmonious relationship between them. As the *yang* element increases the *yin* element decreases, and vice versa. Just as the *yin* element contains the germ of the *yang* element, the *yang* element also contains the *yin* element. The evolution of the *taiji* from *wuji* may be represented by the following diagram (Fig. 2.1).

The *wuji* and *taiji* concepts describe not only aspects of the creation of the universe, but also stages of all relationships between people, between objects, or between people and objects. For example, a room before people enter it is in the *wuji* stage. When people go into the room they bring movements and *taiji* begins. Similarly, the relationship between a person and a piano is *wuji* if the person has no intention to play it. As soon as the intention arises in him to play the piano, *taiji* has begun.

The *taiji* diagram consists of a "double-fish" of different polarity. It illustrates how two opposites can be harmonised into a whole inter-related unit. For example, where there is day, there must be

---

[1]Here, the word "philosophy" is not used in reference to the teachings of such Chinese philosophers as Kongzi (Confucius), Laozi, or Mengzi (Mencius).

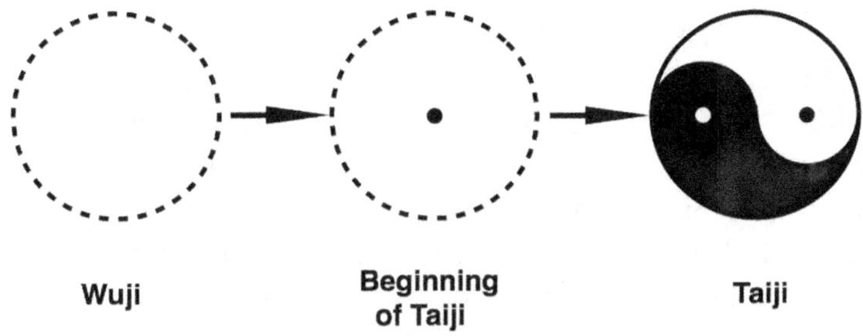

Fig. 2.1   Evolution Of Wuji To Taiji

night and where there is night, there must be day. Day is *yang*, and night is *yin*. Similarly, the sky is *yang*, and the earth is *yin*. Man is *yang*, and woman is *yin*. Heat and motion are *yang*, while cold and stillness are *yin*. This principle is applied to relationships in nature as well as among humans. For example, the negative and positive charges together are needed to produce electricity, just as both *yin* and *yang* are needed to form a *taiji* unity. The husband is *yang*, and needs the wife who is *yin*, to produce the cooperation that is needed in a harmonious family.

The Five Elements or Wuxing
According to Chinese philosophy, the five elements – water, fire, wood, metal and earth – are not inactive matter, but dynamic processes which are basic to an understanding of the natural world. (The usual translation for *wuxing*, "the five elements", fails to convey the idea of movement implied in the Chinese term *xing*.) Water has the properties of soaking and descending (i.e. flowing down). Fire both heats and moves upward (since flames rise into the air). Metal can be melted, moulded, and then hardened. Earth provides nourishment through plants and can be used to build bunks. These five

elements are used to represent different phenomena and dynamic processes. Out of these five elements, four principles are developed based on their inter-relations – mutual creation, mutual closeness, mutual destruction and mutual fear.

According to the principle of *mutual creation*, the five elements produce each other – wood creates fire, fire creates earth, earth creates metal, metal creates water (i.e. it liquifies), and water creates wood. The same pairs of elements are related to each other by the principle of *mutual closeness*. Each element is considered attracted to its source. Thus wood is close to water, water to metal, metal to earth, earth to fire, and fire to wood. The principle of *mutual destruction* describes the series of conflicts between pairs of elements. Wood weakens earth by removing nutrients from the soil. Earth limits water to lakes and seas, and by man-made dams. Water extinguishes fire. Fire conquers metal by melting it. Metal, in the form of axes and knives, can cut down trees and carve wood. Conversely, by the principle of *mutual fear*, an element respects or fears the element which could destroy it. Wood fears metal, metal fire, fire water, water earth, and earth fears wood.

The cycles involving the four principles of mutuality are given diagrammatically in Figure 2.2. The similarities and differences among the principles can be analysed in terms of *yin* and *yang*. Creation and closeness, both constructive principles, are considered *yang*, whereas destruction and fearfulness are viewed as *yin*.

The Bagua or Eight Trigrams
In the principle of *taiji*, the *yang* element is often represented by a line segment or a small white circle. *Yin* is usually represented by two broken line segments or by a small black circle. By combining these two symbols we get a total of four combinations, or forms. Two *yang* symbols together, one placed above the other, is called the great *yang*. A *yin* sign placed above a *yang* sign is called the lesser *yin*. One *yin* sign placed above another is called the great *yin*. A *yang* sign placed above a *yin* sign is called the lesser *yang*. (See Fig 2.3.)

By extending the number of lines to three in each form, we get a total of eight different combinations, each with its own name. (See Fig. 2.4.) These are the basis of the *Bagua*, or Eight Trigrams. The first mythical emperor in Chinese history, Fuxi (29th century BC), is credited as the inventor of the *Bagua*. Fuxi's circular arrangement of the eight trigrams is called the Fuxi, or Xiantian, *Bagua* (i.e. the

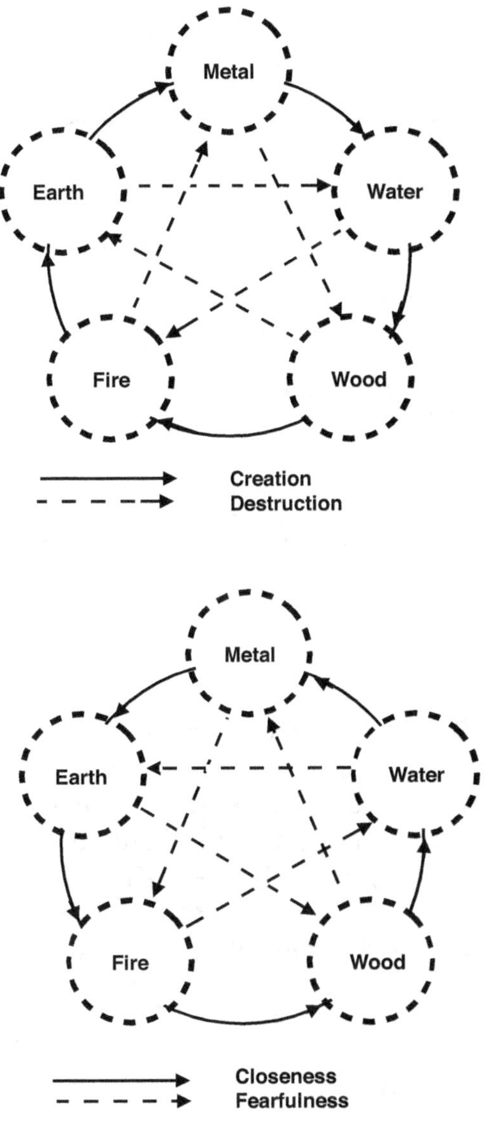

Fig. 2.2 Five-Elements Relationships

Earlier Heaven Eight Trigrams).

There is another arrangement of the Eight Trigrams, called the King Wen, or Houtian (Later Heaven), *Bagua*. According to legend, it was drawn up by King Wen, the founder of the Zhou Dynasty in

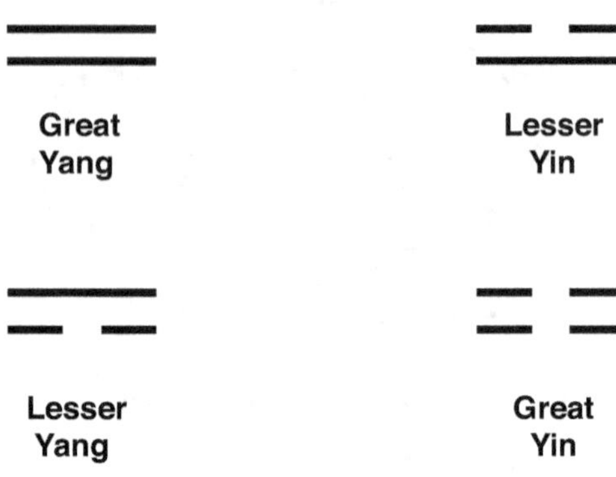

Fig. 2.3   Yin-yang combinations.

around 1143 BC. This sequence of arrangement of the eight trigrams was used to explain the principle of the motion of the universe and was the basis for the development of the Chinese calendar. This is also the *Bagua* that is hung above the front door to ward off bad *qi*.

In the *Yijing* (易经), usually called "The Book of Changes" in English, the number of elements in each form is increased to six, so that a total of sixty-four combinations or forms are obtained. These forms are used in divination.

2.2   Applications

The natural world
The Yin-Yang principle of *taiji* can be applied to every object or situation. We have already mentioned some examples along the way. Another example is this: we can use *yin* and *yang* symbols to describe the relationships among several different nations in terms of population and land. Nations like the United States and China have a lot of land and large populations. Some nations, like Canada, have a lot of land but relatively small populations. A country like Japan

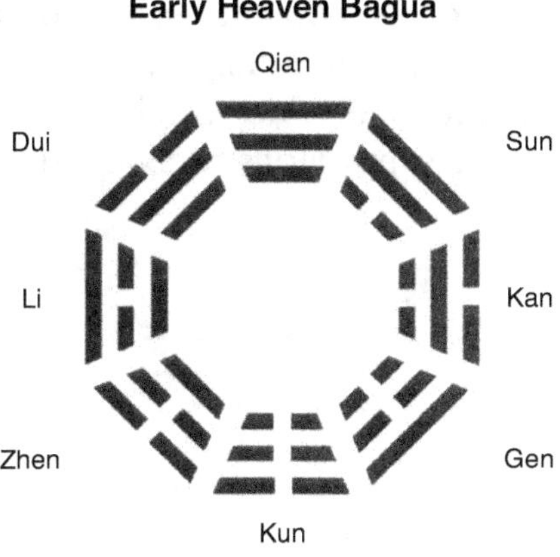

Fig. 2.4 Early Heaven and Later Heaven Bagua

has a dense population and a small amount of land, whereas countries like Iceland are small in both land and population. Since there are only two parameters, the four forms are needed to completely represent the total situation.

Using the lower position to indicate the amount of land (*yang* for large, and *yin* for small) and the upper position to indicate population density (*yang* for dense population, *yin* for sparse population), we get the classification shown in Fig. 2.5. This provides a quick visual understanding of nations which can be translated to predictions of business opportunities, military strategies, etc.

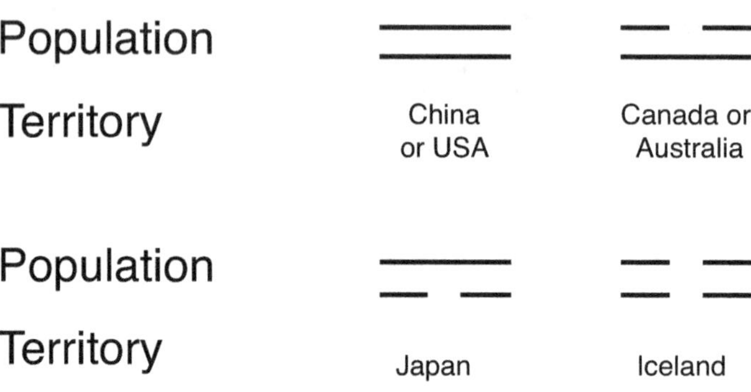

Fig. 2.5   Yin-yang applied to countries.

Medicine
The Five Elements and the Yin-Yang principle are used not only to represent forces in the natural world, but also to provide a basis for the study of physiology, pathology, diagnosis, and therapy in Traditional Chinese Medicine (TCM). Food is classified as "heaty" (*yang*) when it is fried, oily, starchy, or meaty. It is classified as "cooling" (*yin*) if is is steamed, soupy, vegetarian, or fruity. Some fruits full of carbohydrate or protein are "heaty", e.g. the durian, lychee, and avocado. Other fruits that are juicy and sour are "cooling", e.g. mangosteen, apple, and orange. To have good health, one must consume a balance of "heaty" and "cooling" food.

In the human body, the internal organs are divided into two groups: five *yin* or solid organs – viz. heart, spleen, lungs, kidneys, liver – and six *yang* or hollow organs – viz. intestine, stomach, large intestine, bladder, gallbladder, and triple burner, i.e. the space above and below the pericardium. Each of the *yin* and *yang* organs are identified with one of the elements of nature. The heart (*yin*) and the intestine (*yang*) are associated with fire, the spleen (*yin*) and stomach (*yang*) with earth, the lungs (*yin*) and large intestine (*yang*) with metal, the kidney (*yin*) and bladder (*yang*) with wood (see Fig 2.6). (How these pairs of organs are matched, I must confess, is a mystery to me.)

Five Elements	Wood	Fire	Earth	Metal	Water
Directions	East	South	Centre	West	North
Seasons	Spring	Summer	Long Summer	Fall	Winter
Colours	Blue	Red	Yellow	White	Black
Flavours	Sour	Bitter	Sweet	Acid	Salt
Organs	Liver	Heart	Spleen	Lung	Kidney
Sense Organs	Eye	Tongue	Mouth	Nose	Ear

Fig. 2.6 Applications Of The Five Elements

The Five-Element medical model stresses relationships between the organs rather than their individual functioning. Using the principles of *mutual creation* and *mutual destruction*, TCM explains that both an excess, or a deficiency, in one organ may affect another organ. Consequently, problems with one organ may be cured by the treatment of one or more related organs. This approach contrasts with the tendency in Western medicine to cure sickness by treating only the diseased organ instead of considering the whole system or organs within the body. A holistic approach to health is attempted. Since much of the underlying philosophy is unscientific, TCM as a whole has been regarded as pseudoscience.

Martial Arts
There are many styles of martial arts, all of which use the principles

of *yin* and *yang* (or *Taiji*), the Five Elements, and the *Bagua* as the underlying theory, to varying degrees. These principles are not necessary to the trainee if he is interested only in acquiring the basic skills, but they will enhance his understanding of the various techniques and the style of martial arts as a whole. The martial arts may be classified into the External Schools and the Internal Schools. The External Schools concern themselves more with the development of skill in techniques and physical strength, while the Internal Schools concentrate more on the cultivation of the mind and internal power.

The three major Internal Schools are named after the principles that undergird Chinese philosophy: *Taiji quan*, *Bagua zhang*, and *Xinyi quan*. The last of these uses the theory of the Five Elements as its basis. All these Internal Schools emphasise the cultivation of *qi*, or "internal energy". This *qi* is an extension of that which is believed to permeate the universe, and has been called the cosmic energy. The seat of *qi* in the human body is believed to be located in the *dantian*, a point three fingers below the navel and three fingers inside the body. *Qi* is caused to accumulate in the *dantian*, and flow throughout the body along known meridians, by various breathing exercises plus meditation. The expert is believed to be able to transmit his *qi* to others by contact, for the purposes of maiming or healing. The Chinese have identified a total of 136 vital points, or nodes, on the human body which are believed to be vulnerable to attack. Many of these points are used in acupuncture, when needles are inserted to stimulate the flow of *qi* in the body. When closely examined, it will be found that most of these points are in fact parts of the body at which are the concentration of nerves, or where the organs or major blood vessels lie exposed near the surface.

Fengshui

Literally translated, *fengshui* means "wind and water". At its basic level, *Fengshui* is the art of living in harmony with one's environment. (Uppercase 'Fengshui' for the art, and lower case 'fengshui' for the concept.) Man-made objects such as the furniture in the house, buildings, and gardens are arranged or built in such a way as to provide the best blend with the natural environment, with the aim of achieving harmony and prosperity. The art, however, has been developed beyond the basic level to become a form of geomancy that is rooted in Daoist philosophy.

During the Sung Dynasty (1126-1278 AD), *Fengshui* was systematised into the Fujian School which emphasises the use of the relationship of the planets, and the Jiangxi School which emphasises the consideration of *qi* in landscape. The magnetic compass and the principle the *Bagua* were also incorporated in the practice of *Fengshui*. Numerology also features in certain branches of *Fengshui*.

The shapes of many buildings and shopping complexes in Hong Kong are built with the idea of having the best *fengshui*. Chinese people throughout the world look upon a house that faces a road junction as possessing bad *fengshui*. A house that faces a mount or a hill is regarded as having bad *fengshui* because *qi*, and therefore prosperity, is blocked from flowing into the house. Trees blocking the main entrance of the house is also bad fengshui since they are symbolic of joss-sticks on the altar, on which the occupants are going to be sacrificial lambs. Flowing water is regarded as good for *fengshui*, but it must be located correctly relative to the position of the house. A waterfall in front of the house is good, but a river that flows past either the front of back entrance is bad, since wealth will be swept away by the water.

2.3 A Christian Perspective

Some biblical principles must be borne in mind as we come to assess these Chinese arts and philosophy.

God is the Creator and Sustainer of the world
Psalm 24:1-2 say, "The earth is the Lord's, and all its fullness, the world and those who dwell therein. For He has founded it upon the seas, and established it upon the waters." This is the verse quoted by the apostle Paul in 1 Corinthians 10 when he dealt with food offered to idols. (See also Ps. 50:12; 89:11.) Although spoilt by sin, all creation still belongs to our God. The Christian can truly sing, "This is my Father's world."

Chinese philosophy and the Chinese arts arise from, and were developed by, pagans. This, however, does not make Chinese thoughts and discoveries inherently sinful. True, religion has the tendency to colour all aspects of culture, so that in the practice of, say, the martial arts, the trainees have to bow down to the ancestral altars. However, the martial arts in and of themselves are not religious. Today, the armies and police forces of all nations in the world are trained in martial arts that mostly have their origin in Chinese *wushu* (or *Gongfu*). Moreover, many styles of martial arts have been developed into a sport. If a Christian may not practise any form of martial art simply because of its pagan origin, he should not be engaged in other activities that are of pagan origin as well. Where will this lead us to? Football and basketball probably have pagan origins!

We have noted that the *Houtian Bagua* has been used to develop the Chinese calendar. Fishermen use it to determine the tide so as to know when to go out to, and to come in from, sea. Are we to stop them from using the Chinese calendar? The questionable use of the Chinese zodiac as a horoscope in fortune telling, which the Christian would avoid (Lev. 19:31; 20:6, 27), does not mean we should throw away the baby with the bathwater.

The point is that retreat is not the solution to the problems we have to face in the world. Many things in life are not sinful in and of themselves. We must learn to recognise what are cultural in essence and what are inherently religious. The religious trappings may then be separated from the purely cultural. The principles of the *Taiji* and *Bagua*, for example, are capable of being scientifically understood. The *yin* and *yang* elements may be equated with the bits in binary logic, "0" and "1". Those who study computers and mathematics will understand this. The forms of the *Bagua* may then be represented in binary form as shown in Fig. 2.7.

The same can be said of the use of animals in the Chinese zodiac; there should be no problem in using the animals to name the years in the cycle of twelve. When young, I was taught to recite the sequence of the animals in Chinese – first-rat, second-ox, third-tiger, fourth-rabbit, fifth-dragon, sixth-snake, seventh-horse, eighth-sheep, ninth-monkey, tenth-cock, eleventh-dog, twelveth-pig. If I meet someone who is born in the same year as mine, which is the year of the horse, I will know that he is of my age, or twelve years older, and so on. If he is born in the year of the dragon, I will know that he is two years my senior, or fourteen years my senior, and so on. If using the animals of the zodiac to name the years is a problem, then using the names of the week should also be a problem since Sunday, Monday, etc. were names of pagan gods. In the Bible, believers were not required to change their pagan names, e.g. Silvanus was the god of the forest.

Man is commanded to subdue the earth
Genesis 1:28 says, "Be fruitful and multiply; fill the earth and subdue

Trigram	Symbol	Binary System	Decimal System
Quan		0 0 0	0
Dui		0 0 1	1
Li		0 1 0	2
Zhen		0 1 1	3
Sun		1 0 0	4
Kan		1 0 1	5
Gen		1 1 0	6
Kun		1 1 1	7

Fig. 2.7   The Bagua And Mathematics

it; have dominion over the fish of the sea, over the birds of the air, and over every living thing that moves on the earth." The creation mandate requires that we learn as much as we can of God's world, to His glory. In the process, the use of the mind is essential. We are not only to love our God with all our heart, soul and strength, but with our mind as well (Mark 12:30). The apostle Peter tells us that as pilgrims in this sinful world we are to "gird up the loins of your mind, be sober, and rest your hope fully upon the grace that is to be brought to you at the revelation of Jesus Christ (1 Pet. 1:13)."

The Chinese have classified and used thousands of different herbs and minerals, many of which have proved effective in curing many diseases. China, and other countries, are now analysing and studying various herbs by scientific methods to determine the effective ingredients. Even the art of *Qigong* is now being subjected to scientific study. It is a well-known fact that western medicine tend to be particularistic in approach while Chinese medicine tend to be holistic in approach. The two approaches need not be seen as contradictory, but should be treated as complementary. Furthermore, there are certain diseases, notably those of the skin and the nervous system that Chinese medicine seems to be strong in. What is needed is a more scientific approach to the study of these diseases and their cures.

Take, for example, the way a herbal prescription is brewed. We are told to boil the "concoction" in, say, three bowls of water until one bowl of the brew is left, before it is drunk. The combination of herbs in the concoction contains various substances which, when boiled to a certain temperature, and for a certain length of time, will give a certain concentration of medicine just suitable for the particular illness. Instead of saying "three bowls of water is to be boiled until one bowl remains", we should really be looking into the chemical changes that take place under certain temperatures!

When a scientific approach is employed, a lot of the traditional superstitions in Chinese medicine would be removed. The story is told of how herpes, or "shingles" – a virus disease of the nerves – used to be cured by the Chinese. This disease is called "snake" by the Chinese because the red, painful, blisters tend to spread along the nerves, giving the appearance of a snake coiling around that part of the body. The Chinese used to believe that when the snake has coiled itself all around the person's body, he will die. A more accurate way of describing it would be that when the disease has advanced to such a stage that the nerves have been attacked most of the way, death occurs!

Now for the cure. The Chinese used to paint the picture of a tiger's head around the first blisters that appeared with ink that was used in Chinese calligraphy. The popular explanation given for this practice was that the tiger had to be employed to fight the snake! The amazing thing was that the patient often got cured. That was in the old days. When the same cure is attempted today, failure is experienced. The patient has often to be sent quickly to a western-trained doctor. What accounted for the high rate of success in the past and the inevitable failure today? It turned out that the ink used traditionally in Chinese calligraphy was made from the bark of a tree which has medicinal property, while the ink used today is produced synthetically from chemicals!

Because of the absence of a scientific approach, and the lack of proper regulation and standards of practice, many quack doctors exist. Chinese drugs have been known to contain high dosages of arsenic (which is poisonous) and steroids (which have bad side-effects). For these reasons, I must confess that I have more confidence in western medicine than in Chinese Traditional Medicine.[2] I am mindful that Qin Shi Huangdi (d. 210 BC), the First Great Emperor of China, died from an overdose of mercury in his attempt to find the elixir of eternal life.

The duty of living a separated life
The Scripture says: "You were bought at a price; therefore glorify God in your body and in your spirit, which are God's (1 Cor. 6:20)"; "Come out from among them and be separate, says the Lord. Do not touch what is unclean, and I will receive you (2 Cor. 6:17)"; "Abstain from every form of evil (1 Thess. 5:22)". We have advocated a general attitude of non-retreat, of going into the world to study and subdue it. This must not be taken to mean that we are advocating syncretism. Separation from sin, and from anything sinful, is a Christian duty.

We can be too sweeping, however, in classifying many things as sinful simply because that is the easiest way out. Those who condemn *Qigong* as sinful will normally consider the practice of the martial arts and acupuncture as sinful as well. Two basic reasons have been given why the practice of *Qigong* is sinful: first, that it is of pagan origin; second, that it involves meditation, which empties the mind to the possibility of satanic attacks. We have answered the first objection, and will now deal with the second. The so-called meditation of *Qigong* is in reality the practice of breathing exercises in a certain manner, namely by the relaxation of mind and body, concentrating on the *dantian* or focussing the eyes on an object such as a dot on the wall or the green fields in the distance. It is arguable whether it is possible to empty the mind of all thoughts. A person who is awake will always have some thoughts in his mind. In fact, even in the state of sleep, thoughts or dreams occur. The term "emptying the mind" as used in *Qigong* basically means to relax and not to be distracted by worrying thoughts.

The idea of *qi* and its flow around the body is only a model for the explanation of the cultivation of health, endurance, and strength. The apparently amazing feats that the *Qigong* expert is capable of performing need not be attributed to the power of Satan. The expert is able to break a brick with his bare hands, and throw an attacker off powerfully without appearing to exert any effort. These can be explained scientifically. The *Gongfu* expert is trained to harness the strength, weight and momentum of his own body to focus on a point

---

[2]All the figures in this chapter are copied or adapted from Jou, T. H., 1980.

in one swift moment. He is also trained to act with great sensitivity and precision towards the movements of an opponent. He has deliberately cultivated his stamina, poise, and bodily resilience through exercise and breathing techniques. Apart from using body mechanics and motor skills, of which I am certain, my guess is that the expert is able to cause a spurt of adrenalin to flow in his body at the right time. By a combination of such techniques, which he explains by the flow of *qi*, he is able to perform what appear amazing.

People have been known to perform amazing feats in times of emergency. A woman was able to lift up a car that had rolled over her son so that he could be freed. A man was able to knock down a door bare-handed to rescue his children from a burning house. God has given us a wonderful body! While some people surprise themselves by performing amazing feats during emergencies, the Chinese have attempted to deliberately cultivate the ability to do what are normally not possible.

Those who are opposed to the practice of *Qigong* often compare the art to *yoga*. I do not know much about *yoga*. I am, therefore, not in a position to give competent comments on it. *Yoga* is perhaps too closely intertwined with Hinduism to allow the Christian to practice it. However, it will not be surprising to find similarities in the forms and techniques of breathing in the two arts, since China and India have had trade and cultural ties from antiquity. Claims of levitation, "astral travel" (i.e. "soul travel") and other unusual phenomena are to be taken with a pinch of salt. Gross exaggerations are often employed to create an aura of mysticism around the experts of many eastern arts.

What of the wonderful sensations, the sense of well-being, experienced by practitioners of *Qigong*? Sensations there will be, since the practitioner deliberately relaxes himself and engages in breathing exercises which improve the level of oxygen absorbed into the body. Are these sensations inherently sinful? Do we not have sensations of various sorts when we watch a nice show in the cinema, or listen to some beautiful music? Are the nice sensations that arise from the organs of sight and hearing acceptable while those that arise from the organs of breathing unacceptable? As in listening to music, the practice of *Qigong* and martial arts becomes sinful only when one loses control of oneself in the process.

It needs to be said that some forms of *Qigong* do invoke the name of spirits and animals. With such we will have nothing to do.

We are to live to God's glory
The Scripture says, "Whatever you do, do all to the glory of God (1 Cor. 10:31)", and, "See then that you walk circumspectly, not as fools but as wise, redeeming the time, because the days are evil (Eph. 5:15-16)". Life on earth is short. Our days are numbered. We should not waste time in pursuit of things that do not last. We are to seek first the kingdom of God.

The redeemed sinner will no longer wish to parade himself before the world as an expert of *Fengshui* or the martial arts. He would have died to self, and renounced all the vanities of youth and all glory in physical prowess. "Bodily exercise profits a little, but godliness is profitable for all things (1 Tim. 4:8)." Too much time can be spent learning and training in *Gongfu* or *Qigong*. Why cultivate bodily health and power at the expense of living for God? Souls are perishing. The harvest is plentiful, and the labourers are few. We need to think more of evangelism and proclaiming the gospel to the lost.

Furthermore, there are always those who have a weak conscience. We are not to do anything that our conscience condemns us of. "Whatever is not from faith is sin" (Rom. 14:23). If you are unsure whether a particular type of *Qigong* or martial art is good for you, don't practise it. We are not disparaging exercise and the keeping of good health. In fact, it would do many of us good if we pick up a hobby and exercise regularly. All we are saying is that we need to keep things in perspective by living to God's glory.

The sufficiency of Scripture
2 Tim. 3:16-17 says, "All Scripture is given by inspiration of God, and is profitable for doctrine, for reproof, for correction, for instruction in righteousness, that the man of God may be complete, thoroughly equipped for every good work." Scripture is sufficient to guide us in life. There is no need to resort to the study of *Fengshui* before we know how to live harmoniously with the environment and the people in the world. The basics of *Fengshui* are nothing but common sense. A house facing a junction might indeed be dangerous, especially if the road is sloping. An oncoming car might crash into your gates, or your own car might roll away if the hand-brake is not pulled. Moreover, it is never pleasant to have the headlights of passing cars shining into your house at night. Similarly, one who has a weak

constitution should not sleep directly under the fan since he might catch a chill. There is no need to explain things in terms of the flow of *qi*.

Other things about *fengshui* are nothing but *shamanism*, or superstition. A house that has any sharp, rectangular object facing it, whether it is a bus-stop sign or the roof of another house, is regarded as having bad *fengshui*. There was the case of a man who chopped down a tree by the roadside, in front of his house, simply because it was bad *fengshui*. He was issued a fine by the local council. One *Fengshui* expert described the practice as an art, another as a science.[3] The one who called it a science also described it as "a mystical practice that blends ancient wisdom with cultural superstitions"![4]

Christians who are trained in architecture, landscaping or interior-design might have to take into consideration the whims and fancies of their clients. Let your clients consult all the *Fengshui* experts they want. Then adjust your plans to suit your clients' wishes. There is no need for you to ridicule his beliefs, neither is there any need for you to feel contaminated by them.

The same applies to the recent craze in applying the theories in Sunzi's Art of War to business (e.g. Michelson & Michelson, 2003). It is a waste of time for us to delve into a human book originally written for the battle field. We do not doubt the possibility of adapting battle strategies to the business world. For example, it is good strategy to fight your enemy with the back to the mountains. That way, you are facing them only from the front. Moreover, it is easier to fight downhill than to attack uphill. Similarly, it is good in business to operate with a strong sponsor behind you, who acts as "the mountain behind you".

The Christian, however, will find the broad principles of Scripture sufficient to guide him even in business. There is no need to produce tomes on how Christian principles should apply in the business world. After all, we are not attempting to christianise the busi-

---

[3]Of course, we are not saying that anything accomplished by a scientific approach necessarily makes it true or right. Wrong presuppositions might be adopted which would lead to wrong conclusions. All we are saying is that the adoption of a scientific approach eliminates superstitious beliefs by the application of the mind to observable facts. Furthermore, we are not claiming that all western-trained doctors are not superstitious. Many of them are as pagan as other people!

[4]Albert Low and Lillian Too both call it an art in their books. Lillian Too called it a science elsewhere. See: Too, Lillian, 1995. The Sun Magazine, April 9, p. 19.

ness world, nor any other institution, like what the Reconstruction-ists tried to do. Our aim is only to live a godly life while we have breath. After that will be the life in glory.

2.4 Conclusion

The Bible teaches that man is made in the image of God. It also teaches that man is fallen. In the Chinese culture, we find human genius and human depravity combined in the most intense way. The genius and the resilience of the Chinese people are well-known throughout the world. But the depraved side of the Chinese is also well-known, The Chinese are perhaps the only people, as a people, known for the habit of spitting everywhere. Just a generation ago, a sputum could be found under every table in a Chinese coffee-shop to cater for this habit of the Chinese. And who has not heard of the Chinese eating almost everything under the sun – cockroaches, snakes, the brain of live monkeys, human foetuses eaten as a tonic, etc.?

I was discussing the Chinese culture with some friends once. One of them pointed out that the classical Chinese songs and stories always contain the notes of sadness and tragedy. I did not ask which songs he meant. Perhaps he meant songs like *Man Jiang Hong* (满江红, "The Fury of the Swollen River")[5], and *Wang Zhaojun* (王昭君).[6] I did not ask which stories he meant. Perhaps he meant stories like *Hong Lou Meng* (红楼梦, "Dream of the Red Mansion") and *San Guo Yan Yi* (三国演义, "Romance of the Three Kingdoms"). But I am inclined to agree with him. There is always a plaintive note of helplessness and hopelessness in these songs and stories. This reminds us of the account of Ishmael in the book of Genesis. He was dying... and weeping... (Gen. 21:16-17).

We must understand that Chinese culture is basically a culture corrupted by sin. It needs to be redeemed. Chinese philosophy is bankrupt human wisdom. We have noted that the Chinese are a hard-working, resilient, and intelligent people. Spiritually, however, there is a void in them. The Chinese people need the gospel of "Je-

---

[5]For a translation of the poem, see: Wong, Andrew W. F. For the song, see Man Jiang Hong.

[6]Wang Zhaojun was one of the four well-known beauties of ancient China who was married off to the king of the Xiongnu Empire (Mongolia) in order to establish friendly relations with the Han dynasty (206 BC-8 AD). For the story of Wang Zhaojun see Yuan, Haiwang (2003). For the song, see Wang Zhaojun song.

sus Christ and Him crucified". The challenge to us, Christians, is to understand the Chinese people, and to bring the gospel to them.

Questions

1 Ah Kow has been interested in Chinese martial arts from young. He trained conscientiously in many styles of *Gongfu* and is quite an expert in it. He hears the gospel and is converted. His Christian friends begin to advice him to stop practising *Gongfu*, causing Ah Kow to be confused and sad. How would you counsel him?

2 Mr. A graduated as an architect and works in a well-known firm. He encounters a difficult client who is constantly changing the plan of his new house because he consults various *Fengshui* experts about the location, orientation, and shape of the house. How should Mr. A react to his client? Is there the possibility that he might compromise his faith?

3 Should a Christian indulge in listening to Chinese songs? What if some of the songs have lyrics praising Buddha? Should we adopt some Chinese hymns by translating the lyrics into the language used in our church?

References

1 Bavinck, J. H. 1961. An Introduction to the Science of Missions, Presbyterian & Reformed Pub. Co.

2 Jou, Tsun Hwa. 1980. The Tao of Tai-Chi Chuan. Tai Chi Foundation, N. J. An intellectually satisfying exposition of the theory and practice of the *Taiji* martial art.

3 Low, Albert. 1993. Feng Shui. Pelanduk Pub.

4 Man Jiang Hong song: https://www.youtube.com/watch?v =gIQ2JxF_Kis. (Last accessed, March 2020.)

5 Michaelson, Gerald A. & Michaelson, Steven. 2003. Sun Tzu For Success. Adams Media.

6 Ong, Hean-Tatt. 1991. This is a fascinating study of the meaning and significance of the *Bagua*, linking the origin of the Chinese people to the biblical account of creation, the tower of Babel, the flood of Noah's time, and the monotheistic worship of Shangdi, the one true God.

7 Palmer, Martin, ed. 1990. T'ong Shu: The Chinese Almanac. Vinpress.

8 Ross, John. 1990. The Origin of the Chinese People. Pelanduk Pub.

9 Sun Zi's Art of War, Canfonian Pte. Ltd. 1992.

10 Too, Lillian. 1993. Feng Shui. Legenda. The books come in four self-contained illustrated volumes, the substance of which are clearly and attractively presented. The first volume is sufficient to provide the beginner with an idea of what Fengshui is all about. The fourth volume discusses numerology in Fengshui.

11 Wang Zhaojun song: https://www.youtube.com/watch?v=nSKI8yUlqB8. (Last accessed, March 2020.)

12 Wong, Andre W. F. http://chinesepoemsinenglish.blogspot.com/2010/05/yue-fei-river-all-red.html. (Last accessed, March 2020.)

13 Yuan, Haiwang: https://people.wku.edu/haiwang.yuan/China/tales/zhaojun_b.htm (Last accessed, March 2020.)

Three

THREE FACTORS THAT BIND THE CHINESE (Tit. 1:10-16)

Just as the Cretans of Paul's time had developed certain cultural characteristics that were not very flattering (Tit. 1:12-13), so also the Chinese down the centuries. One from a background of the Chinese Religion will face tremendous struggles when confronted by the claims of Bible. If not for the irresistible grace of God in Jesus Christ, no Chinese will be converted. Of course, the same can be said of the people of other cultural backgrounds. However, what are the peculiar factors that hinder the average Chinese from yielding his life to Jesus Christ? Three hindrances are discernible, viz. pietism, maxims, and materialism.

3.1   Pietism

By pietism is meant here the strong sense of loyalty the average Chinese feels towards his religion, family and clan. This sense of loyalty may either be conscious or unconscious in the individual. The Chinese Religion has been passed down from generation to generation in his family and he finds it difficult to renounce this heritage. Age inspires reverence and the length of time the Chinese Religion has been practised in the family generates a veneration for the religion that is otherwise hard to account for. Tradition dies hard.

The immediate family is closely linked to many other families of the same surname. These families constitute the clan. Daughters are married out to families of other surnames while sons marry the wives in from other families and so promulgate the surname of the clan. Unity in the clan is visibly established by the *gongsi* (公司) or *huiguan* (会馆), an association whose members meet in a building which houses the ancestral altar of the clan. A record of the family tree is kept by the association. The Chinese name normally consists of three monosyllable words, the first of which is the surname, followed by the generation-name and then the individual's personal name. The middle or generation name is taken from a poem of the clan. One generation would use one word from the poem, the next generation would use the next word and so on, until the last word is reached, when the cycle would be repeated. When two persons of the same surname meet, they can determine the generation that each belongs to from their middle names. The one who is of the younger generation would have to call the other "Uncle", "Granduncle", or even "Great-granduncle". The situation sometimes arises when one who is older in age has to call another younger in age "Uncle" or "Granduncle"!

To the Chinese, the honour of the family name must be preserved at all cost. If dishonour is brought to the family by any individual in it, the family is said to have *lost face* in the sight of other people. In other words, the family has been put to shame – a shame that is very strongly felt because the Chinese fear being looked down upon by the public. This *face* is not limited to the level of the family, but comes down to the level of the individual. For example, to belittle a person in public is to make him *lose face* and this is virtually unforgivable.

While it is true that many young families today are not members of their clan-association, neither do they follow the generation-poem when giving names to their children, the sense of loyalty to their families is still very strong. The oldest son in particular would feel obliged to carry on the family traditions. If the eldest son happens to be the black-sheep of the family and does not bother with carrying on the traditions, the next son in line would feel obliged to do so. When none of the sons carry on the traditions, and the parents are not worshipped when they die, the family *loses face*. An eldest son who becomes a Christian is regarded as being unfilial to his parents and disloyal to his family. It does not matter much if the younger ones in the family become Christians. Eldest sons who have become Christians often meet with severe opposition from their families.

3.2 Maxims

Maxims are widely accepted rules of conduct which concern certain generally accepted truths. It is not often realised that Chinese maxims constitute a considerable force that controls the conduct of the Chinese. These maxims are often embodied in short, pithy sayings. Maxims bind the Chinese-educated person in that they provide him with a ready-made view regarding people, events and conduct, as well as guidance for behaviour in different circumstances. Thus a Chinese-educated person feels self-sufficient, even self-satisfied. When a Chinese-educated person is challenged by the gospel to repent of his sin and to believe in the Lord Jesus Christ, he would often hide behind a saying such as, "Rivers and mountains can be moved, but a man's disposition cannot be changed" (江山易改，本性难移). It is our purpose here to examine how true are the truths expressed in these sayings.

In every culture in which there is a well developed spoken and/or written language, a body of wise sayings is bound to develop with time. China is one of the oldest civilisations in the world and, as would be expected, numerous such sayings have developed. Moreover, Chinese is a living language, that is to say, it is a language that is still widely used, is suitable for use in various spheres of education, and is constantly undergoing change. As such, some newer sayings have emerged that were not heard of by the older generations.

It would be readily agreed that it is Chinese culture that has given rise to Chinese sayings. The Chinese sayings in turn, affect the conduct of the Chinese and so also mould Chinese culture. It is well known that the Chinese are a very hardy and persevering people. The tenacity of overseas Chinese has not only evoked admiration but also envy and fear among other peoples in some parts of the world. This characteristic of the Chinese is reflected in the saying, "Where there is determination, even solid gold or rock can be broken" (精诚所至，金石为开). Its English equivalent is "Where there is a will, there is a way". This is expressed pungently in Chinese in a sentence which consists of two four-word parts.

Hence, in every part of the world where there are Chinese, they are noted for their industry both in business and in studies. The Chinese people are found to be owners of sundry shops, restaurants, take-away shops and launderettes in Southeast Asia, America, Europe, Scandinavia and, in fact, in every part of the world where there are Chinese. In the sphere of education, the Chinese community in any nation often top the list of those who pass in any examination. The largest percentage number of people holding Ph.D. degrees in any one community in the U.S.A. are supposed to be Chinese. Surveys made in the U.S.A. and in the U.K. show that the Chinese (together with the Japanese) do better than their Caucasian counterparts in studies (Eysenck and Rose, 1979).

Another factor that influences the emergence of wise sayings is the geographical location of the Chinese civilisation. China is a mountainous country and this is reflected in sayings such as the one already quoted above, "Mountains can be moved, but a man's disposition cannot be changed". The tiger was one of the many animals that roamed the mountains of China and this has given rise to sayings such as, "If the tiger's lair is not entered, how can the cub be caught? (不入虎穴, 焉得虎子). This latter saying is equivalent to the English, "No pains, no gains".

As has been alluded to above, time is the next factor that influences the growth of sayings. An example of a modern Chinese saying is, "To hit is to show affection, to scold is to show love" (打是疼, 骂是爱). This is often shortened to "To hit is to love" (打是爱). It is often hard to pin-point the source of such sayings. They most probably come from the pen of some present-day authors. The movies certainly popularise these sayings worldwide, as has happened with the mistaken English saying, "Love means never having to say sorry". (Mistaken, because I believe that the saying expresses a falsehood. Love often means that we *have* to say sorry to our loved ones whom we have wronged.)

While on the subject of movies, we should note that the particular type of Chinese *wuxia* fighting stories (武侠小说) which has been very popular among the Chinese for a long while has played a significant part in inculcating Chinese values, maxims and ancestral worship. These stories come in long series of a few volumes each. With their standard themes of family feuds and revenge, they depict the exploits of fighting men and women of olden day China. The stories have been made into video (and now internet) films, each series often consisting of many episodes, each of at least 45 minutes of viewing time.

How true are the maxims expressed in these Chinese sayings? We have examined some such maxims and discovered that they were influenced by culture, geography and time. Chinese maxims are the product of the Chinese culture which is located in its particular geographical location, and these two factors change with time. The overseas Chinese of today live in different geographical locations in the world as compared to their ancestors who lived in China, and various changes in their culture are noticeable. For example, the Chinese in South-east Asia build many temples and celebrate religious festivals in a big way whereas only a few Chinese families in the Chinatowns of Britain have altars in their homes. While Chinese maxims express the wisdom of the Chinese people, it should be recognised that they are only the products of man. As such they can never claim, either individually or collectively, to embody absolute truths.

Mountains can be moved, but a man's disposition can also be changed, if he is willing to be changed. One should not hide behind a man-made saying in order to continue in sin.

The tiger's lair should be entered if the cub is worthwhile catching, but not when the cub is worthless and harmful. For example, one should not risk the harm that comes from lying, stealing, smoking or committing adultery just for the sheer pleasure of the experience.

While difficulties hindering worldly success can be overcome by self-determination, the solid rock of sinful and self-willed living, hindering one from yielding one's life to Jesus Christ, can only be broken by the power of the Holy Spirit.

To correct a child with the rod is right and is in fact taught in the Bible, e.g. "He who spares his rod hates his son, but he who loves him disciplines him promptly" (Prov. 13:24). However, to beat a wife into submission is certainly not a loving act.

3.3 Materialism

Materialism controls the life of the Chinese more than any other factors. Whenever Chinese people meet, their conversation almost always revolve around the subjects of money and food. Prosperity in times past was measured by the number of sons a person had. That was when most Chinese were farmers and sons were needed to help with farming. Nowadays prosperity is measured by how much money a person earns, how much property he has and how well he eats. Speak to any Chinese, and you would soon discover how money-conscious he is. He talks about money, he schemes to earn more, and he dreams of how to win more. The various gods are not worshipped for their attributes (such as their holiness, justice, mercy, or love because they have none of these attributes) but for their supposed ability to help a person win the four-digit-lottery.

Materialism constitutes a hindrance because the average Chinese seeks after material wealth and has no time to seek to know God. Living a Christian life is "time-consuming" to him. Moreover, being a Christian would mean that he cannot carry out the occasional corrupt practices that are so necessary to quick prosperity.

We appreciate the fact that our forefathers left China to eke out a living overseas. We have eaten the fruits of their labour and we are what we are now because of their toil. However, it cannot be denied that most overseas Chinese today are not as poverty-stricken as their forefathers. They live to earn and accumulate more. It would have been quite all right if it were just a matter of working hard for their livelihood. What is pitiable is that their whole beings are saturated with the desire to be materially prosperous so much so that there is no room for any desire to be spiritually wealthy. To work hard is good, but greed is idolatry and is condemned by God (Col. 3:5).

The Bible does not teach that money is evil in and of itself. Rather, it teaches that the love of money is a root of all kinds of evil (1 Tim. 6:10). Many would have experienced this and found it to be true, but many never seem to learn. Many rich men have found that their lives are empty and unhappy despite their wealth. It is interesting to note that it was food that caused Adam and Eve to fall. They ate the fruit of the tree of knowledge of good and evil, which had been forbidden them by God (Gen. 3). It was also the desire for food, a red stew, that caused Esau to sell his birthright (Gen. 25:19-34; Heb. 12:16-17).

God wants all men to be saved and to come to a knowledge of the truth (1 Tim. 2:4). Not all men, however, will turn to him to be saved. Those who turn to trust in Jesus Christ for salvation are received by God as His children. They are heirs of God and co-heirs with Christ (Rom. 8:12-17). Sad to say, many people prefer to have the red stew of this world rather than eternal life in Jesus Christ.

> Do not worry, saying, 'What shall we eat?' or 'What shall we drink?' or 'What shall we wear?' But seek first the kingdom of God and His righteousness, and all these

things shall be added to you (Matt. 6:31, 33).

3.4 The Sum Of The Matter

All the three hindrances to faith in Jesus Christ described here are present in the Chinese to varying degrees. Pietism is stronger in the Chinese who is aware of it, understands it and is proud of his heritage. It is not so strong in the Chinese who has not given any thought to it. Maxims bind the Chinese-educated Chinese more than they do the Chinese who is Western-educated or one who has had a national-education in the country of his abode. Of the three hindrances, materialism is the strongest in any Chinese.

Pietism shows the Chinese clinging to the traditions of men. Maxims show him to be worldly-wise and self-righteous. Materialism shows him to be covetous and loving the things of this world. In other words, the Chinese is no different from any other people in the world. Western people are of the Caucasoid stock. They have pale skins, sharp facial features and sunken eyes. The Indians are of the Indo-Dravidian stock. They have sharp facial features like the Caucasians, but are dark instead of pale-skinned. The Africans are mostly of the Negroid stock. They are dark like the Indians, but have curly hair, thick lips and large flat noses. The Chinese are of the Mongoloid stock. They are yellow-skinned, have flat faces with high cheek-bones, and almond-shaped slanted eyes. All are different physically, but all are the same in nature. All are sinners in the sight of God. All need the Saviour. The Chinese do need Jesus Christ.

Questions

1 When approached by a Christian, what are the common objections raised by the non-Christian if he is bound by (a) pietism, (b) maxims, and (c) materialism? How would you answer his objections?

2 Christians are, in a sense, also bound by maxims, namely, the teachings of the Bible. Is there any value in memorising Bible verses and using them when witnessing to the Chinese?

3 What other hindrances can you think of which hinder the Chinese from receiving the gospel? Are they actually different manifestations of the three hindrances studied here?

Reference

1 Eysenck, Hans and Rose, Steven. 1979. Race, Intelligence and Education. New Scientist. 15 March, pp. 849-852.

Four

THE ANSWER TO MAN'S NEED (Acts 17:16-34)

O ne who has just become a Christian needs to be assured that faith in the Lord Jesus Christ is indeed the ultimate answer to his deepest spiritual need. This chapter is intended to help the believer who is new in his faith. What are the things that make Christianity unique and different from the religion he has come out from? We consider here some of the unique characteristics of the Christian faith.

4.1   The Bible Is True

Do absolute truths exist? Is there an infallible measure of what is good and what is bad, of what is right and what is wrong? These questions are relevant to our discussion.

We have seen that the Chinese Religion is only a religion invented by man to meet the needs of man. Such a religion is called a *natural* religion. Since it has its origin in man, it cannot provide clear, and infallible, guidance on spiritual matters. With the Chinese, it has been a case of "the blind leading the blind" through the many centuries. The seeming peace and well-being experienced by devotees are necessarily transient. The only lasting things the Chinese Religion contributes to its followers are a fear of the unknown spirit-world and superstition.

In contrast, the Christian faith is a *supernatural* religion. This means that it has its origin in God and everything centres around God. Instead of man groping to find out about God, God has revealed Himself to finite man so that he may now know what God is like. God's revelation is recorded in the Bible through the instrumentality of chosen men. "Prophecy never came by the will of man, but holy men of God spoke as they were moved by the Holy Spirit" (2 Peter 1:21).

Massive external evidences exist, including those of science, history, archaeology, geology, etc., which support the claim that the Bible is true.[1] However, it is not our purpose here to try and prove the truth of the Bible. The Bible speaks for itself and needs no humans to prove its authenticity. The Spirit of God will guide the humble seeker to understand and accept the truths in the Bible. The believer is content to know that the Lord Jesus Christ accepted the Scripture (the Old Testament) as God's Word (Luke 24:27, 44; John 10:34, 35). He is content to know that the Lord personally commissioned His followers to write the New Testament (John 14:26; 15:26; 16:13; Gal. 1:12; Eph. 2:20).

Since the Bible is God's word, it provides an infallible measure of what is good and what is bad, and of what is right and what is wrong. Absolute truths are only found in the Bible and they are not altered by man's ideas. The Bible is sufficient to guide us in all matters of faith and practice. "All Scripture is given by inspiration of God, and is profitable for doctrine, for reproof, for correction, for instruction in righteousness, that the man of God may be complete, thoroughly equipped for every good work" (2 Tim. 3:16-17). Man may choose to follow or not to follow these truths, but truths they will always be.[2]

4.2   Salvation Is Needed

The Bible reveals to us who God is, and what He is like. It shows us also what man is like, and what he has done in relation to the truths about God. We shall consider some of these truths.

---

[1] See, for example, McDowell and McDowell, 2017; Morris, 1988.

[2] See, for example, Edwards, 1978. An explanation of the inspiration and authority of the Bible.

God created and sustains all things, including human beings. Since God is our Creator and Sustainer, He has every right to our lives. We owe God everything that we are, and everything that we have, whereas God does not owe us anything. As such, God deserves our worship and He does demand that we worship Him, and Him alone. To worship other so-called gods is to offend our Creator badly.

God is holy and just. His holiness is such that He cannot accept anyone with even a spot of filthiness. His justice is such that every sin needs to be punished. The character of God is reflected by the law He has given to men. This is summarised in the Ten Commandments (Exodus 20:1-17). The breaking of even one small point of the law is regarded as the breaking of the law as a whole and will disqualify one from entering heaven (James 2:10). This is what has been happening ever since the first man and the first woman, Adam and Eve, sinned against God. The sinful nature of Adam and Eve has been passed down the human race. All of us sin against God in thoughts, words, and deeds. We are all guilty before our Creator!

God is love and He is forgiving. He is not just a loving God but He is Himself love. He is merciful to undeserving sinners and will always forgive the repentant sinner. Since the God of the Bible is the only true God, He alone is capable of showing perfect love and mercy. The love of God is seen supremely in His sending of Jesus Christ, His only begotten Son, to this earth to save sinners from eternal damnation in hell. We have offended God, our Creator. God has sent His only begotten Son to save us by His death on the cross and His resurrection from death. That is true love!

The Chinese take pride in their long, unbroken, civilization. The written history of China stretches back 4,000 years. The oral history of China stretches back another more than 2,000 years, making a total of over 6,000 years. Songs such as "Descendants of the Dragon"[3] and "My Chinese Heart"[4] stir the hearts of many Chinese around the world, not so much because they desire to live in China or are unhappy with wherever they have settled, but simply because it touches the inner emotional core of their being. At some stage in life, a Chinese person would be enquiring about his/her own ancestry. The system of naming one's children practised by the Chinese, and the meticulous way family records have been kept by the clan, have enabled many individuals to trace back their ancestry many generations – often to more than ten generations. However far one traces his ancestry, there comes a point when he asks, "Where did the Chinese come from?" "How are we related to other ethnic groups?" "Where do human beings come from?" The satisfaction derived from tracing one's ancestry many generations back is only temporary. We soon are confronted with the doubts and dissatisfaction of ignorance of our past.

This is where the Bible comes to our help. It is revealed that human beings are descended from Adam and Eve, the first man and the first woman created by God (Gen. 1:26-31; 2:18-25). When the descendants of Adam and Eve sinned badly against God, the great flood occurred which killed everyone except Noah's family of eight persons (Gen. 6-10). From Noah's family, the world was populated again. The arrogance and rebellion of men against their Creator caused God to confuse their language so that they scattered over the earth (Gen. 11). Attempts have been made to trace the ancestry of the Chinese to the sons of Noah (e.g. Wang and Nelson, 1998). Although it would seem impossible to trace the ancestry of the Chinese with certainty this far back, there is the comfort of knowing from the Bible where the Chinese came from, and how the human race began. No religious books and ancestral records in the whole world gives a more satisfactory account of the origin of the human race than the Bible.

What about the theory of Evolution and the evidences of science? Do they not give an alternative explanation of the origin of the human race, and of the universe? While science has improved the living conditions of man tremendously, it is unable to offer convincing proof of the so-called theory of Evolution. The teaching of Evolution should rightly be called a hypothesis, not a theory, for it has never been proven scientifically. Many assumptions have been made and many inconsistencies have not been explained (Baker, S., 2003; Morris, 1998). If anything, science has shown the credibility of human descent from one common ancestry. The advances of science have not been able to explain the cause(s) of, nor provide a cure for, human depravity.

The Bible shows that ever since our forefather, Adam, rebelled against God, this rebellious nature has been in us. We choose to walk out on God, and to worship the gods of our own creation instead.

---

[3] Hou Dejian, 1978.
[4] Wong, James and Wang, Fuling, 1982.

Our sinful nature manifests itself in the things we do – lying, stealing, hating, thinking filthy thoughts, and hordes of other things. Is there any person who can claim he has not sinned against God? All men sinned in Adam. As a result, death came to all men (Rom. 5:12-21). All men sin against God. As a result, "The wrath of God is revealed from heaven against all ungodliness and unrighteousness of men..." (Rom. 1:18). The Bible reveals the need of man to be saved from his sin.

4.3   The Lord Jesus Christ

The average Chinese thinks that the Christian faith is just another religion, and that the Lord Jesus Christ is worshipped as a deity similar to the Chinese gods. The believer needs to have a clear understanding of who Jesus Christ is and what He has accomplished.

Unlike the many Chinese gods which are merely legendary or mythical characters produced by the pen of men, Jesus Christ was a real historical person who lived in Palestine about two thousand years ago. Time and time again, the Bible has been proved to be a reliable history book. It does not record the history of all the nations of the world, but it records the historical events which pertained to God's plan of redeeming the world. Jesus Christ lived on this earth during the time when the Roman Empire stretched from Britain across to Europe, down to North Africa and eastward to North India. This period corresponded to the Han Dynasty (206 BC-220 AD) in China. The Bible gives a vivid account of the life of Jesus Christ and the growth of the early church during this period of Roman rule. Apart from the Bible, secular historical records exist which mention Jesus Christ during this period. One of these is the account of Flavius Josephus in his history book entitled "The Antiquities of the Jews". Josephus was a Jewish priest as well as a historian, and he worked for the Roman army as an archivist for a time. Another reference to Jesus Christ is found in Tacitus's book called "Annals". Tacitus was a Roman historian.

Having established that Jesus Christ was an actual historical person, we need to remember also that He was not just a good man who has been deified and worshipped, as has happened to the Chinese deity Guan Gong. Jesus Christ is the divine Son of God who is presently reigning in heaven and interceding for believers. He existed from eternity as God (John 1:1-18). He took on perfect human nature when He was conceived by the power of the Spirit of God and born to the virgin Mary. In His earthly life, He performed many miracles and was raised from death after being crucified. All these show that He was not just human but also divine. The Church has always believed that Jesus Christ is one person having two natures.

> It is, therefore, true faith that we believe and confess that our Lord Jesus Christ is both God and Man. He is God, generated from eternity, from the substance of the Father; Man born in time from the substance of His mother. Perfect God, perfect Man, subsisting of a rational soul and human flesh. Equal to the Father in respect to His divinity, less than the Father in respect to His humanity. Who although He is God and Man, is not two but one Christ.
> *The Athanasian Creed*

Jesus Christ was a historical person. He is divine, and not merely a person who has been deified. What was the purpose for the divine Son of God to come to this earth and take on perfect human nature? The Bible gives us the answer, "Christ Jesus came into the world to save sinners" (1 Tim. 1:15). This is a truth revealed to us in the Bible. Just as animal sacrifices of oxen and lambs were offered up to God by the Jews before the coming of Christ, His death on the cross was the perfect sacrifice that takes away the sin of His people (John 1:29; Matt. 20:28). By faith in Jesus Christ, the sinner is reconciled to God. His sins are forgiven and the righteousness of Christ is counted as his (2 Cor. 5:21). He is identified with Christ in His death and in His resurrection (Rom. 6:5). He enters into the privileges that belong only to those who trust in Jesus Christ, which among other things include:

i the privilege of communion with God, by the indwelling Spirit, through the reading and study of Scriptures, through prayers, through fellowship with God's people, and through sharing in Christ's suffering while living out the Christian life;

ii the privilege of serving God, through proclaiming the gospel and acting as salt of the earth and light of the world;

iii the privilege of having eternal life, and having the fear of death removed, knowing that believers will be raised from the dead and given a resurrection body to dwell in heaven, and there to worship and serve the Lord for all eternity.

4.4 Certainly Unique

What have been given above should be sufficient to convince one of the uniqueness of the Christian faith. Faith in Jesus Christ is certainly the answer to man's deepest spiritual need. The Lord had said, "I am the way, the truth, and the life. No one comes to the Father except through Me" (John 14:6). It will be most foolish of the believer to ever entertain any thought of turning back to his old way of life.

We conclude this chapter by mentioning some other differences between the Christian faith and other religions. Other religions teach salvation by works, i.e. by human effort at doing good, while the Bible teaches salvation by grace, i.e. unmerited favour, mercy shown by God to undeserving sinners (Eph. 2:8-9). Through faith in Jesus Christ alone, a believer is forgiven by God his sins and regarded as righteous in His sight (Rom. 3:28). Other religions either deny the need of a mediator or advocate the need of many mediators which are the spirits and gods of the religions. The Bible teaches that there is only one mediator between God and men, namely Jesus Christ (1 Tim. 2:5). Other religions teach some form of ritual prayers or worship which require the devotee to face a certain direction or a visible representation of a god. The Bible teaches that God is Spirit and we must worship Him in spirit and in truth (John 4:24; Exodus 20:4).

"Whoever calls upon the name of the LORD shall be saved" (Rom. 10:13). Dear reader, are you saved?

Questions

1 There are Chinese Christians who feel sad that they have lost part of the Chinese culture. What would you say to them?

2 Various attempts have been made to explain the origin of religion. Three main methods are:
(i) The Historical Method: Religions as they exist today may be traced back to a primitive origin. The development has been influenced by environment.
(ii) The Psychological Method: Certain factors in man, such as

fear, instinct, a feeling of independence, etc., combined and cooperated with man's natural environment to give rise to religion.
(iii) The Theological Method: God exists and has revealed Himself. Man is created in the image of God, so that he has the capacity to understand and respond to the objective revelation of God. Man, therefore, seeks after God, but because of sin is unable to do anything pleasing to God unless influenced by God's special revelation (the Bible) and enlightened by the Holy Spirit.
(See Van Til, 1974.)

We can trace the origin of various elements of the Chinese Religion by a *historical method*, but this does not mean we have explained the existence of the religious consciousness in the Chinese. Which of the above methods explains this? Is the Chinese Religion an improvement of a primitive religion or is it a degradation of an original *high* religion?

3 How important is the teaching on life after death to the Chinese? Why? What are the important points regarding this teaching which you will seek to bring across?

References

1 Baker, Sylvia. 2003. Bone of Contention. Biblical Creation Society.

2 Edwards, Brian. 1978. Nothing But The Truth. Evangelical Press. An explanation of the authority and inspiration of the Bible.

3 Ham, Ken and Hodge, Bodie. 2016. A Flood of Evidence. Master Books.

4 Hou Dejian, 1978. *Long De Chuan Ren* (龙的传人). https://www.youtube.com/watch?v=L8kLPuBSruc. (Last accessed, March 2020.)

5 McDowell, Josh and McDowell, Sean. 2017. Evidence That Demands A Verdict: Life-Changing Truth for a Sceptical World. Thomas Nelson.

6 Morris, Henry M. 1988. Many Infallible Proofs: Evidences for the Christian Faith. Master Books.

7 Van Til, Cornelius. 1974. An Introduction to Systematic Theology, Presbyterian and Reformed Pub. Co.

8 Wang, Samuel, and Nelson, Ethel R. 1998. God and the Ancient Chinese. Sinim Bible Institute.

9 Wong, James and Wang, Fuling, 1982. *Wo De Zhong Guo Xin* (我的中国心).
https://www.youtube.com/watch?time_continue=91&v=HFdfljqRfBY&feature=emb_logo. (Last accessed, March 2020.)

Five

LIFE WITHIN THE CHINESE CULTURE (Col. 2:16-23)

Before we consider some facets of Chinese life and see how the Christian should conduct himself, some general comments are in order. One who claims to be a follower of Christ should live a distinctive Christian life. The Christian must not adopt the values and moral standards of the world. He should not entertain any thought of compromise with the world.

This does not mean, however, that we no longer have anything to do with the world. On the contrary, we are to remain in the world at the same time that we remain separate from the world. The Christian is to be the salt of the earth (Matt. 5:13). This means that he has to check the decay of moral values in society by his presence and influence. The Christian is also to be the light of the world (Matt. 5:14). This means that he must lead an exemplary life in which godliness and righteousness are clearly seen. He bears witness to Christ by life as well as by words, with the view that the spiritually blind will be led to Jesus Christ.

5.1   Now That You Are A Christian

When a person is converted, his old nature is transformed and made new. The process of renewal continues through the life of the believer. There are attitudes and actions which belong to his old self that need to be *put off*, and there are other attitudes and actions which belong to the new self that need to be *put on* (Col. 3:9-10; Eph. 4:22-24). We discuss here certain things peculiar to the Chinese Christian that need to be *put off* and *put on*. He must *put off* his connection with past idolatry, and he must *put on* obedience to the Lord's command to get baptised.

A believer should have nothing to do with astrology, sorcery, divination or consulting the spirits of the dead. All these are detestable to the Lord (Deut. 18:10-13). The Christian should not keep any amulet or charm. The yellow strips of paper obtained from mediums must be destroyed. Lockets with pictures of idols must be broken and thrown away. Chinese people often wear jade pendants that are in the shape of idols. If the Christian is wearing one, it is suggested that he sends it to the jeweller's to have it ground into some other ornamental shape.

We are here referring to the personal belongings of the believer. We are not saying that the believer should practise iconoclasm, that is, to go around breaking idols and destroying other objects of worship that are not his own. It would be unwise for the Christian to suggest to his parents that the family altar and idols should be destroyed as they have not come to faith in Christ. This will only provoke a strong negative reaction towards the Christian faith, not because of "the offence of the cross" but rather because of the natural defensive instinct in them being aroused. Also, there is the danger of denying the gospel of "justification by faith" by giving them the impression that certain deeds on their part – in this case, the destroying of the idols – are necessary before they can be saved. We must insist that "faith comes by hearing, and hearing by the word of God" (Rom. 10:17). The word of God preached is more powerful than any double-edged sword and will cut asunder their ties with family traditions. Not only that, it will cut asunder the grasp of Satan upon their lives. It is when they have experienced the saving power of Christ in their lives that they are made willing to destroy objects that would otherwise hinder their spiritual growth (cf. Acts 19:13-20). Turning to the true and living God, of necessity, involves turning away from idols (1 Thess. 1:9).

The believer is a new creation who is indwelt by the Spirit of God. He is now free from the power and reign of Satan. "He who is in you is greater than he who is in the world" (1 John 4:4). It is important for the Christian who has formerly been offered to a Chinese god as a 'god-child', to grasp this fact. The Bible declares that "the wicked one does not touch him" (1 John 5:18). Satan cannot recapture the man who is kept by Christ. The believer need not fear that any spell or charm will be cast on him. Any spell or charm will not work on a true believer. This is not to say the believer should drop his guard against attempts to bewitch him. Evil spirits have no power to indwell a believer or to take control over his mental faculty. The believer, however, is still a mere mortal as far as life on earth is concerned. He can be harmed physically by potions taken orally or by the fumes of burnt substances breathed in. Potions and burnt substances feature prominently in occult practices. (See also Appendix 2.)

Another matter that concerns the new believer is baptism. The Christian should seek baptism from the elders of his church soon after his conversion (Matt. 28:19; Acts 2:41; 8:36-39). Chinese parents often mistakenly associate baptism with the point at which a person becomes a Christian. To them, it is the point of no return when their son or daughter would be bound forever to be a Christian. For this reason, some parents would allow their children to go to church but would forbid them from getting baptised. Such a situation often provides the opportunity for the Christian, or his friend or pastor, to explain the gospel to them.

A commonly encountered problem is opposition from an aged parent or grandparent to the Christian's baptism. When the life of the aged parent or grandparent is endangered because of his fury over the matter, it is probably wise to delay getting baptised. The Christian should make it known to him, however, that is for his sake that the baptism is delayed.

To delay baptism for the sake of someone whose life may be endangered is one thing. To delay baptism when the Christian is afraid to make an open declaration of his faith is another. The heart of man is very deceitful and the Christian should guard against giving excuses because he is ashamed to be identified with Christ. The Lord Jesus Christ said, "He who loves father or mother more than Me is not worthy of Me. And he who loves son or daughter more than Me is not worthy of Me" (Matt. 10:37).

5.2   The Single Christian And His Parents

The average Chinese who has just become a Christian may over-react to the system of filial piety that he has been brought up in. In a Chinese family, the mother is often the one the children can confide in and she acts as the middle-person between father and children. The father is treated as the absolute monarch of the family to whom is rendered cold, mechanical and sometimes grudging acts of obedience. There are, of course, exceptions to this, but I believe this is a correct description of the situation in many families.

As Christians, we reject the system of ancestral worship. We worship God, and God alone. It should be noted, however, that the Fifth Commandment, which requires that the Christian honours his father and his mother, still applies, whether the parents are Christians or not (Deut. 5:16). We honour our parents by being obedient to them as far as possible, by caring for them and by consulting them when making any major decision. It has been well said that it is better to honour our parents while they are living rather than when they are dead. Instead of sullen obedience to the parents, there should be a warmth that allows for natural conversation to take place. It is in such an atmosphere that spiritual things can be discussed in order to expose the parents to the gospel. Too many Christians, though concerned for the salvation of their parents, fail to cultivate this warmth. As a consequence, they find it so difficult and awkward to discuss spiritual things with them.

5.3   Courtship And Marriage

Marriage is an important event in anyone's life and Chinese parents would be the first persons to worry when their sons or daughters are not married by the age thirty. Christian girls often find the pressure more acute, especially in a situation where the Christian girls far outnumber the Christian men. There have been instances when parents advised their daughters not to become Christians until they are married.

Whatever the problem may be, the Christian should not court someone who is not a Christian. Courtship means getting to know each other better with the possibility of marriage in mind. It is a scriptural command that believers are not to be unequally yoked with unbelievers (2 Cor. 6:14; cf. Ezra 9:2, 12; Neh. 13:23-28). All types of relationship that the believer establishes with others need to be examined in the light of this command. We note, however, that the closest possible union between two persons is marriage. It follows that this command is particularly applicable to the marriage relationship. A lot of heartache and sorrow can be avoided if relationship with an unbeliever of the opposite sex is not allowed to develop in the first place. God means us good by forbidding such an unequal union. When husband and wife are both Christians, they share the same outlook on life and have the same priorities. This is not possible when one is a Christian and the other is not. It is no wonder that Christians who disobey God at this point never lead truly happy married lives.

Another reason why God forbids such an unequal union is because His honour must be preserved. There is a tendency for us to be man-centred in our thinking. We think more of our good and forget that God's honour is at stake. When we become Christians we are no longer our own. We are bought at a price (1 Cor. 6:19, 20; 7:23) – a price that has been paid with the blood of Christ (Acts 20:28; 1 Peter 1:18, 19). The Christian is a new creation (2 Cor. 5:17) and when he or she marries an unbeliever, the new creation is united with the spiritually dead unbeliever (cf. Eph. 2:1). This is dishonouring to God (cf. Mal. 1:6; 2:11,12).

What can we say to one who is converted after he has begun courting an unbeliever? We need a lot of wisdom and sensitivity to deal with such a situation. It is an extremely painful thing for the believer concerned to break off the relationship. Only one who has gone through a similar experience can truly appreciate the pain involved. However, the command not to marry an unbeliever still applies. The believer may want to help the unbelieving partner to come to a saving faith in Christ by continuing the friendship with him or her. He should beware, however, of making this the excuse for continuing the relationship which in reality he does not want to break with. There is also the possibility that the unbelieving partner may follow him to church faithfully and with time profess some sort of belief, when in fact no true conversion has taken place. The human heart is deceitful above all things and these warnings should be heeded. A true Christian is someone who has made up his mind to forsake even loved ones and follow Christ (Matt. 10:37-38). The believer should make his position clear to the unbelieving partner, explaining in all kindness the reasons for his stand. Emotions run high at this stage and the Christian must make every effort to ensure that these do not smother his rational faculty.

God is not just an idea in the Christian faith. He is real and He is all that the Bible claims Him to be. He will definitely chastise His disobedient children. He withdraws His blessings when we sin. It is far better to be obedient and not to court an unbeliever. Should it happened that you are unable to find a Christian life-partner, and singlehood comes to you, remember that you have renounced marriage (with unbelievers) because of the kingdom of God (Matt. 19:12). The single life can still be a very fulfilling one (cf. 1 Cor. 7:32-35; Mark 12:25). Why not start praying daily for God to provide you with a Christian husband or wife?

It may be that the reader is a Christian who has already married a non-Christian. You may be wondering what you should do. The first thing that can be said concerns your attitude of heart. In the face of what the Scripture teaches you should recognise that you have sinned against God. If you harden your heart and become resentful, you only increase your guilt and, therefore, also increase the wrath of God upon you. You should rather be sorrowful over your sin and confess it to the Lord. The mark of a true Christian is that he is repentant and submissive towards God after he has committed any sin. Divorcing the husband or wife who is not a Christian is definitely out of the question as this would be contrary to what the Lord teaches in Matthew 5:32 and which is reiterated by the apostle Paul in 1 Corinthians 7:11-13, 39. Once the sin is confessed, it has been forgiven. Our heavenly Father is merciful and forgiving, and he does not want us to live a joyless Christian life burdened with the remembrance of sin forever. "If we confess our sins, He (God) is faithful and just to forgive us our sins and to cleanse us from all unrighteousness" (1 John 1:9).

By way of some positive teachings, we shall examine the following passages of Scripture to see how they apply to the Christian who is already married to an unbeliever:

   i *Relationship between husband and wife*: Ephesians 5:22-33 in its
     context applies to Christian families, but the principles are relevant here. The wife is to submit to her husband and respect him whether he is a Christian or not, with the assumed proviso that the demands of the husband are not contrary to the law of God.

The husband is to love his wife whether she is a Christian or not. (See also 1 Pet. 3:1-7.)

ii *The situation is not hopeless*: 1 Corinthians 7:12-16 in its context applies to the case of one who has become a Christian after he or she is already married, but the principles are again relevant here. The Christian husband or wife, by his or her faith and witness, may be the means by which God would use to convert the unbelieving partner and the children in the family. Good may still come in spite of, not because of, your sin and disobedience.

iii *Bringing up the children*: Ephesians 6:4, Proverbs 22:6 and Deuteronomy 4:9-10 are passages which urge Christian parents to teach the word of God to their children in order that they may know the way of salvation and godly living. The Christian husband or wife should ensure that the children grow up under godly influence and are exposed to the teachings of the Bible. (See also Mark 10:13-14.)

5.4   The Married Christian And His Parents

A Christian couple would normally marry in a church. They should not pray to the ancestral altar when they get home. The custom of exchanging jewellery and cakes before the wedding takes place is harmless. So also is the custom of serving tea to parents and relatives during the wedding, provided the couple do not kneel down to them. The tea ceremony is, in fact, a good way for the Christian couple to visibly acknowledge their indebtedness to their parents and to honour and respect them on such an important occasion.

In the Old Testament, bowing is an attitude of respect and reverence. The orientals, in the presence of kings and princes, often prostrate themselves upon the earth. Bowing is frequently noticed as an act of religious homage to idols and also to God (Unger, 1974:153). By the time we arrive at the New Testament, kneeling before a person implies strongly that one is worshipping him (Matt. 2:11; 4:9; Mark 15:19). The cases of bowing before people in the Old Testament should, therefore, not be taken as a rule of conduct for Christians. Mordecai refused to kneel down to Haman who was a high official in the king's court (Esth. 3:1-5). The apostle Peter refused to allow

Cornelius to kneel to him (Acts 10:25, 26). Even the angel of God forbade the apostle John to bow to him (Rev. 19:9, 10; 22:8, 9).

Even if the Christian has no intention of worship in his heart, he should avoid bowing down to a person for the sake of the conscience of onlookers. The early Christians understood the implications of bowing down to people, and preferred martyrdom to worshipping the Roman emperors. (See also Appendix 3.)

In old China, the male children married their wives into the same house and the father remained head of the house. When the household became too large, or when both parents passed away, the household broke up and separate family units were formed. Among overseas Chinese, this practice is seldom adhered to. The children often work far from home and they prefer to start their own families. It falls on the lot of the eldest son to take the parents under his roof.

The biblical ideal is for the man to leave his parents and start a new family with his wife (Gen. 2:24; Eph. 5:31). This separation should not be pressed to the point of neglecting the parents. Eastern Christians find that they have to break away from their parents in order to conform to the scriptural ideal of having separate family units. The individualism of Western society, however, has produced broken family units in which the parents are not cared for. The aged parents are often sent to old people's homes. To Chinese people, this is a cold and uncaring solution which they find unacceptable. There are situations in which the family has not much choice but send the aged parents to certain nursing homes. Thankfully, there are more and more nursing homes in many countries that are operated with a warm and caring atmosphere. Young families should continue to visit, care for, and provide for their parents even though they are not living together.

It may be difficult for the eldest son to let his parents live on their own. Tradition is strong and if the parents do not object to living separately, it would be the relatives who object. The Christian should ensure that he exercises headship in his house. This need not lead to any strained relationship between the two parties if problems are resolved with sensitivity and love, and if a warm relationship has been cultivated with the parents.

A slightly different situation arises when the eldest son works near to his parents' home and is obliged to live with them. In this case, the Christian has to exercise headship over his own family, although he is not head of the household. Being head of his own family does not mean that his parents cannot advise him on family matters. Neither does it mean that there should be a barrier between them as far as relationship is concerned. There can still be a natural warmth between them. The Christian and his family should still respect them as their elders. It does mean, however, that he has the final say on matters relating to his family. The Christian may not be able to live a physically separate life from his parents but there should be an emotional separation from them. It should be the wife that he turns to first, instead of his parents, when there is need for emotional support. The wife is to be looked upon as a helper and not as a mother-substitute (Gen. 2:20). This may seem like stating the obvious, but it is a fact that many men who appear to be big and strong are still emotionally tied to their mothers' apron strings after marriage.

The friction of living together often causes quarrels to occur between the wife and her mother-in-law. The husband must not automatically side with his mother out of loyalty to her. His loyalty should be to his wife and, if anybody, it should be the wife whom he sides with. The wife is not married into the family to be a household chattel. She is married in to be the queen of the family. She should be loved, cherished and protected as the husband's better half. "For this reason a man shall leave his father and mother and be joined to his wife, and the two shall become one flesh" (Eph. 5:31). However, both husband and wife must seek to live peaceably with the parents (Rom 12:18; James 3:17,18).

We would not venture to say more than these, for fear of being idealistic and impractical. Christian families often find that they have to bear up with inconveniences caused by situations that are less than the biblical ideal. We can only hope that the next generation of Christians do not have to face so many of the same problems.

What have been discussed above may appear negative and defensive. This attitude of mind should not prevail in Christians. We should rather have a positive attitude towards our parents, and attempt to extend our love and care to them. Peace in the Bible is active, and not passive. In Hebrews 12:14, Christians are urged to pursue peace with all men. The N.I.V. conveys the active sense of the original more clearly by rendering the verse as, "Make every effort to live in peace with all men".[1]

---

[1]Whenever the meanings of original words and phrases are sought, Strong's

Unlike Western people, Chinese parents are never impressed by children who say they love them. Chinese people are not given to expressing love to their parents by words or by physical expressions such as hugging or kissing. These are simply not acceptable within Chinese society. Parents, however, look upon gifts in the form of money or food as expressions of love. Therefore, when we visit our parents, it is good to bring along some fruits or cakes. Even if your parents protest and say that you should not have bothered bringing the things, you should continue to do so each time you visit them. In the socio-cultural context of the Chinese, a "No" often means "Yes, thank you". During the Chinese New Year, or on their birthdays, it is good to give them *hongbao* (red envelopes containing some money) as a token of our love. Many a strained relationship in the family would not have resulted had Christians been less miserly in giving these gifts. It has become customary also for the sons to give some money from their salaries each month to their parents. Christians must make sure that they do not fail in this area.

It takes the first generation of Christians to show forth a warmer relationship between family members, in which the children are able to communicate with the father freely, and hugs and holding hands on special occasions are common. Unconverted relatives might feel uncomfortable or frown upon this, but they know that it is not within their area of concern. One suspects that many of them are impressed, and even envious, of the relationship in the Christian family. Social norms should be adhered to as far as possible. We must teach our children to address their grandparents on both sides of the family correctly. Dialect groups differ in the way they are addressed. On the man's side, the grandparents may be addressed as "Yeye" (爷爷) and "Nainai" (奶奶) and those on the woman's side as "Gonggong" (公公) and "Popo" (婆婆). In the Fujian dialect, the grandparents on the father's side are referred to as "Laigong" (内公) and "Laima" (内婆) while those on the mother's side are "Guagong" (外公) and "Guama" (外婆) – the "Lai" and "Gua" meaning 'within' the family and 'outside' the family, respectively. (We have noted that the wife is regarded as being married into the husband's family.) Not many Chinese men are blessed with much facial hair, but it is imperative that a man shows respect to his father and father-in-law by not growing a beard if they do not have a beard, or not growing a beard longer than that of any

---

and Vine's have been consulted.

one of them, while they are living.

Any parent who may be reading this book should have realised that a Christian is not trying to be awkward nor to break the hearts of his parents, but rather to live a life that is pleasing to God. God's ways are always best for us, whether we are Christians or not. It is hoped that this book would contribute towards creating better understanding between parents and their Christian children. A Christian yearns for his parents to come to a saving faith in Christ because he loves them.

Questions

1 Parents will begin to worry when their children are not married by age thirty. Christian girls often find the pressure more acute. What do you think are the reasons for this and how may they be overcome?

2 Ah Kow is getting married. His unbelieving parents insist on consulting a medium to find a good date for his marriage. What would you say to Ah Kow?

3 Mr. A has been courting Ms. B for some years. Ms. B then becomes a Christian. What would you say to her if she comes to you for advice?

4 Ms. C is going out with a non-Christian man. A sister warned her about the danger of being unequally yoked. Ms. C answers by saying that she knows of a number of cases of unbelieving husbands and wives who were converted after marriage, and that she feels that it is all right for her to marry an unbeliever. What would you say to Ms. C?

References

1 Strong's Exhaustive Concordance of the Bible, with Greek and Hebrew Dictionary. Crusade Bible Pubs. Inc.

2 Unger's Bible Dictionary, 3rd Ed. Moody Press.

3 Vine, W. E.. Expository Dictionary of the New Testament. Oliphants.

Six

OFFERED FOOD AND FESTIVALS (1 Cor. 10:1-11:1)

We consider here the vexed question of food offered to idols, Chinese festivals, and the Christian attitude towards these. The question is, "Should we participate or should we not; and if we do, or do not, to what extent?"

There is the simplistic and pragmatic approach advocated by some people who would have no qualms about eating food that has been offered to idols, because "an idol is nothing" (1 Cor. 8:4), and "the earth is the LORD's, and all its fullness" (1 Cor. 10:26, 28). This approach is simplistic because it fails to take into account the nature of the Chinese Religion as a whole and the implications of such an approach. It is pragmatic because this is the easiest way out for the Christian and does not consider other aspects of the biblical teaching on this matter. Those who advocate this approach would teach that we may freely participate in the various festivals, regardless of the things done in connection with the festivals, as long as we do not actually burn incense and bow down to the idols.

Then there is the over-scrupulous and pharisaic[1] approach which teaches Christians to keep clear of food offered to idols and all Chinese festivals. This approach is over-scrupulous because the Christian is constantly on the look out for things to avoid doing or to destroy. It is pharisaic because it begins with the Scriptures but builds upon them teachings that are far from the meaning and the spirit of those very Scriptures. Carried to its logical conclusion, the Christian who follows this approach will have to cease to be Chinese!

We shall here attempt a biblical approach that is applied directly to some practical situations in the Chinese culture. The Bible passage of direct relevance to us is 1 Corinthians 8:1-11:1. (See also Appendix 4.) Our intention here is to bring out the sense of the passage and not to give a detailed exposition of the various verses. Of the commentaries consulted, I have found "The Wycliffe Bible Commentary, (Moody Press)" most helpful.

6.1   1 Corinthians 8:1 - 11:1

All the verses from Chapter 8:1 to Chapter 11:1 belong together and cover the subject of food sacrificed to idols. The "food sacrificed to idols" were the remainders of animals sacrificed to heathen gods. Whether an animal was offered as a private or a public sacrifice, portions of the meat remained for the offerer. If offered as a private sacrifice, the flesh might be used for a banquet, to which were invited friends of the offerer. If offered as a public sacrifice, the meat left after the magistrates took what they wanted might be sold to the markets for resale to the people of the city. The problems, then, were these:

i Might a Christian partake of meat offered to a false god in a heathen feast?

ii Might a Christian buy and eat meat offered to idols?

iii Might a Christian, when invited to the home of a friend, eat meat which had been offered to idols?

To guide the believer in these problems, Paul first sets forth the general principles in Chapter 8. In Chapter 9 he illustrates the principles. In 10:1-11:1 we have the admonition and application to the Corinthians.

---

[1]This word is used descriptively, and not in a derogatory sense.

General Principles (8:1-13)

8:1. Christians do possess knowledge, but it may be only superficial and incomplete. Knowledge, in addition, is not sufficient for the solution of all problems, for by itself it puffs up. Love, on the other hand, builds up.

8:2. While here on earth, man's knowledge of God is always incomplete.

8:3. To love God brings both a knowledge of God and a sense of God's knowledge of the individual.

8:4. An idol cannot really be a representation of God. How could wood or stone represent God's incorruptibility?

8:5. The apostle admits, however, that there are those called gods and lords.

8:6. Yet for us there is but one God, the Father, who first created all things and for whom we, the new creation, live. And there is but one Lord, Jesus Christ, who was the agent responsible for God's creation and is still the agent responsible for the new creation.

8:7. From here to the end of the chapter Paul expounds the words, "love builds up" (v. 1). This is necessary because not everyone has in him the knowledge that there is only one God and one Lord, which enables one to eat offered meat without harm to the conscience.

8:8. Paul points out that meat in itself will not bring believers near to God.

8:9. In the next few verses Paul warns the strong to be careful that their liberty (i.e. the exercise of their rights) does not prove a stumbling block to the weak. In other words, knowledge will not solve the problem (cf. vs. 1-3).

8:10. The person with a weak conscience will be embolden to eat offered food because of seeing you eating in an idol's temple. "Be embolden" (literally, "be built up") is ironic. Fine edification this is; it builds up to sin!

8:11. The reason why the strong believer has become a stumbling block is introduced. When the weak brother, for whom Christ died, persistently violates his conscience by eating something he thinks he should not, he sins.

8:12 The worst consequence of this matter is that the strong believers sin against Christ in sinning against the brethren. The argument is based on the unity of the body of Christ.

8:13 Paul concludes by saying that if there is any possibility of a weaker brother being caused to stumble, he will abstain from eating the offered meat.

Illustration Of The Principles (9:1-27)
Paul does not diverge from the subject here. Rather, he illustrates the principles just set forth by an appeal to his own experience. As an apostle and one who also possessed Christian liberty, he could claim financial support from those to whom he preached (vs. 1-14). However, he refused to exercise his rights in order to gain a reward. His highest pay is to preach without pay (vs. 15-23)! Such a decision demanded personal discipline and privation (vs. 24-27). The Corinthians, of course, were to apply the lesson of self-denial and discipline to the problem of meat sacrificed to idols.

Admonition And Application (10:1-11:1)
Paul concludes his discussion of meats offered to idols with admonition (vs. 1-13) and application (10:14-11:1). In the application he deals with participation in heathen religious festivals (vs 14-22), with the eating of meat sold in the market place (vs. 23-26), and with the eating of meat in a private home (10:27-11:1).

10:1. Paul has emphasised the need of personal discipline and the possibility of failure in the realm of rewards for the undisciplined. To show the reality of the possibility, he uses the nation Israel as an illustration of failure, and with this illustration he admonishes the Corinthians to "be careful" lest they fall also. But first Paul must enumerate the Jew's advantages. The first privilege was that they "were all under the cloud", i.e. they were under prolonged supernatural guidance. "They all passed through the sea", which points to a supernatural deliverance, the second privilege.

10:2. The third privilege was their union with their leader, Moses, who under God provided them with supernatural leadership.

10:3. The eating of the manna, the spiritual (or supernatural) food, was the nation's fourth privilege.

10:4. Supernatural sustenance was Israel's fifth privilege. "The same spiritual drink" refers to the events mentioned in Exodus 17:1-9 and Numbers 20:1-3. Since the people of Israel obtained the water in the opening years of their wilderness wanderings and in the closing years, it is only natural to infer that Christ, the Supplier of the water, was with them all along the way.

10:5. One might think that such privileges must mean success. Not so with Israel. Privileged people may experience divine displeasure. Actually, only Caleb and Joshua survived the displeasure.

10:6. The first reason for Israel's failure was that they lusted (cf. Num. 11:4), preferring the food of the world, Egypt, to that of the Lord, the manna.

10:7. They also became idolaters, the second cause for failure (cf. Exodus 32:1-14, 30-35).

10:8. The third reason, sexual immorality, is a reference to the incident involving Israel and the Moabite women (cf. Num. 25:1-9). The 23,000 who died is not a mistake, although Moses wrote the number 24,000. Paul's "one day" should be noted. He refers to those slain by the plague in one day, while Moses' figure includes the ones who died later from the effects.

10:9. Presumption was the fourth reason (cf. Num. 21:4-9). They dared God to live up to His promise to discipline if they doubted His word.

10:10. The fifth reason was that they grumbled (cf. Num. 16:41-50). Paul may be alluding to the Corinthians' attitude to their own spiritual leaders in the matter of idol meats (the other four reasons can be linked with this problem).

10:11. The events were examples, and the written accounts of the events were warnings for us. Believers in this age are to reap the benefits of preceding ones.

10:12. A word of admonition is given to the self-assured, the strong who have no thought for the conscience of the weak. Be careful lest you fall into God's discipline, and thus become disqualified (cf. 9:27).

10:13. A word to the discouraged, who feel that the Christian life is so hard that they can never hope to survive its trials. The temptation you are faced with is only one that is common to man. God will not let you be tempted beyond what you can bear. A way out will be provided, not to escape, but to endure in the midst of temptation.

10:14. The application follows. Heathen religious festivals are considered first (10:14-22). The command to flee from idolatry might surprise the ones who prided themselves on their liberty, but Paul commands the use of the way of escape immediately. To the weak, Paul has just been assuring them of God's help in time of temptation. Now he wants them to see that that does not give them licence to dally needlessly with it. Flee from it!

10:15. The readers are sensible enough to judge what is said.

10:16-17. Participation (or sharing) in a Christian religious table involves fellowship with the being to whom the worship is directed, namely Christ. The apostle explains why. Partaking signifies a share in, or union with, the deity.

10:18. The example of Israel (now a Jewish religious table) confirms the fellowship of the worshippers with the deity.

10:19-21. The example of Gentile festivals follows. The offered meat and the idols remain what they are. Though the idols and things sacrificed to them are nothing, yet they are used by demonic forces to lead men away from the true God (cf. Deut. 32:17, 21). Believers are united to the Lord and not to demons. They are not to partake of the food offered to idols at a heathen feast.

10:22. Will the Corinthians arouse the Lord to jealousy as their fathers did? Can they risk His anger with impunity?

10:23. Meat bought in shops is now considered. Paul repeats the general principle of liberty, subjecting it to the principle of benefit and edification (cf. 1 Cor. 6:12).

10:24. Nobody should seek his own good, but the good of others.

10:25-26. Permission is here granted for eating any meat sold in the market. No troubling of the conscience by the asking of questions about the meat is necessary.

10:27. Finally, the apostle considers the case of private dinner parties in the homes of unbelieving friends. The believers may eat without raising questions of conscience.

10:28. But if anyone should nudge the believer and say, "This has been offered in sacrifice", then he is not to eat for his sake. The believer must voluntarily respect the weaker conscience.

10:29-30. Paul explains the action. What good is there in his eating if it means his liberty is blamed? How can grace, i.e. thanksgiving for the food, be said for that which offends a brother?

10:31. The principle that is all-inclusive in the entire discussion is introduced. The glory of God is the ultimate aim.

10:32. The good of others comes next, whether they are Jews, Gentiles or Christians.

10:33-11:1. Paul concludes with the example of himself, in that he seeks the good of others, with the ultimate aim that they might come to a saving faith in Christ. He can boldly offer himself as the Corinthians' example, but for the one reason that he imitates Christ.

6.2   Food Offered To Idols

From the above explanation of 1 Corinthians 8:1-11:1, a few things are clear. First, idols are nothing more than inanimate objects of the materials from which they are made (8:4; 10:19). They have no power to cause harm nor to do good. Other Bible passages confirm this (Isa. 44:6-20; Jer. 10:1-5 ; Psalm 115:4-8). Chinese idols are often made from plaster-of-paris, cement or porcelain; or they may simply be paintings or writings on paper, cloth or stone tablets. Occasionally, they are made from wood or some plastic materials. However hideous they may look, the Christian should not fear them.

The idol in and of itself is one thing, the worship of the idol is another. There are spirits behind the idols being worshipped, though not the ones their worshippers thought. When men sacrifice to idols, it is never a neutral activity that has no meaning. They are in fact sacrificing to evil spirits (10:20 cf. Deut. 32:17). In other words, it is possible for Satan to extend his influence to the system of worship as a whole. Satan is only too ready to exert his influence wherever men refuse to submit themselves to God. Systems of thought and religions can be permeated by such influence. The minds of men can be captured and drawn away so that they become darkened and cannot see the light that is in Jesus Christ (2 Cor. 4:4).

Satanic influence must not be ruled out when we consider the Chinese Religion. Strange phenomena are often observed when mediums go into a trance. These phenomena cannot be of God because God will never associate Himself with such idolatry. The Scripture teaches that the devil is on the prowl and evil spiritual forces are at work (1 Peter 5:8; Eph. 6:12). The Christian must never get himself involved in the worship of idols (10:14).

Are Christians to eat food that has been offered to idols? The answer depends to a great extent on the occasion that the food is consumed. The food that has been offered to idols is, in fact, not changed. It remains to be food and has not become 'spirit infused'. Whether we eat the offered food or not makes no difference to our standing with God (8:8; 10:19). It is when the food is eaten in connection with a religious feast that the Christian may not partake. "The Lord's table" reminds us that the Lord is the host at the sacrament. By parity of reasoning "the table of demons" indicates that there may be other hosts (10:21). To share food in such a situation is to establish fellowship with demons (10:20 cf. Acts 15:29; 21:25; Rev. 2:14, 20 and esp. 9:20).

It follows that the Christian may buy and eat any food that is sold, whether in the market, in the shops, or in the restaurants (10:25). Chinese people offer mostly cooked food to idols. It is unlikely that the Christian will buy uncooked meat in the market that has been offered to idols. It is possible, however, that some of the cakes he buys from Chinese shops and stalls, and some of the food he eats in Chinese restaurants, have been offered. This is particularly so on festive occasions. The Christian is to give thanks to God for the food and eat without raising questions of conscience (10:25, 30; 1 Tim. 4:4-5).

Similarly, when invited to a meal in a friend's home, or to a non-religious feast, we are to give thanks for the food and eat without raising questions of conscience. However, if someone were to point out that the food has been offered to idols, we are to abstain for his sake (10:28). "All things are lawful for me, but all things are not helpful, all things are lawful for me, but all things do not edify. Let no one seek his own, but each one the other's well-being" (10:23-24).

We should note, however, that altars and idols are found in the homes of the Chinese as well as in the temples, and religious feasts are held in the homes as well as in the temples. This makes things difficult for the Christian, who may be the only believer at home. The food that has been offered to the idols in the home on a festive occasion is eaten together by the family during meal times. To share food in a situation like this is to enter into fellowship with demons. Moreover, the believer would be spoiling his witness to his unconverted family by eating the offered food. It is the nature of the Chinese Religion to be accommodating and this should be reason enough for the Christian to be watchful and not to compromise. We should become all things to all men so that by all *possible* means we might save some (9:22; 10:33). (This is the intended meaning of the texts, as the NIV makes clear. Compare with 9:23-27.) An action that is against a biblical command and that does not advance the gospel is not a possible means for the believer.

What then should the Christian do? He should explain his position to his parents and ask for some food to be set aside for him before the rest of it is offered to the idols. Many Christians have found their parents very understanding and willing to meet the request.

We may summarise our stand as follows. The Christian may NOT eat offered food *in connection with a religious feast or meal* because:

i the food that is sacrificed is, in fact, sacrificed to demons;

ii he must preserve a clear witness to his unconverted family;

iii believers with weak conscience might be caused to stumble in their spiritual lives.

It is worth noting that some parents have been attracted to the Christian faith because of its simplicity of worship, where no food is offered.

6.3   Chinese Festivals

The Chinese calendar is divided into twelve lunar months and a number of festivals are celebrated in a year. We shall list here the major festivals together with a brief description of what each of them is meant to celebrate, before considering the Christian attitude towards them.

1. 1st month, 1st-15th days: Chinese New Year

This is also referred to as the Spring festival (春节). The story goes that a monster called *Year* (年) used to come once every twelve months to devour people and cause destruction to houses and properties. It so happened that on one such occasion, a boy who wore red clothes was spotted by the monster. The monster was afraid of the red colour and did not dare to come near the boy. When the boy threw a fire-cracker at the monster, it ran away in fear. Seeing this, other people began to beat drums, cymbals and empty tins to frighten it off once and for all. From then on, the Chinese began celebrating that occasion as the Chinese New Year. Fire-crackers are burnt and drums and cymbals are beaten in merriment. Red becomes the colour of good luck and prosperity. The seasons are divided into *years* after the name of the monster. Red envelopes containing some money are exchanged on this happy occasion to welcome the new year.

2. 1st month, 9th day: Birthday of the God-of-heaven

The God-of-heaven (*Tian Gong* (天公) or *Yu Huang Shangdi* (玉皇上帝)) is the highest deity in Daoist reckoning and his birthday is celebrated by offering food and burning joss-sticks and joss-papers at the front of the house on the eighth mid-night of the first month. The Hokkiens (Fujian-speaking people) also offer whole branches of sugarcane in thanksgiving to the god for protecting their ancestors when they were hunted down by the Mongols. The people in the Fujian Province of China hid in a large sugarcane plantation when they were pursued by the Mongols. They managed to survive in there for many days because the sugarcane plants not only provided refuge but were also a source of nourishment.

3. 1st month, 15th day: End of Chinese New Year

This is also known as *Chap Goh Meh*, i.e. "the Fifteenth Night" (after the Chaozhou dialect), or *Yuan Xiao Jie* (元宵). The end of the Chinese New Year is celebrated mainly by the people from the province of Guangzhou. They include the Cantonese as well as the Teochews (Chaozhou-speaking people). Teenage girls would throw oranges into rivers at night and lanterns, often in the shape of lotus flowers, are let down to float in the river as well. This practice is believed to augur well when prospective husbands come looking for them. It is seldom seen nowadays, although there are attempts made to revive it – more as a tourist attraction. Instead a feast is held at home or in a restaurant, when a sweet dessert of glutinous rice balls is served.

4. 3rd month: All Souls Day or Qingming (清明)
The date for this festival varies each year, falling around the month of April. It is a time of remembrance for the deceased. The tombs of the deceased in the cemetery are cleared of weeds, the inscriptions on the tomb-stones are repainted and food is offered.

5. 5th month, 5th day: Rice-dumpling Festival or Duanwu Jie (端午节)
An emperor who reigned during the Warring States period (475-221 BC) was advised by his general Qu Yuan (c. 340-278 BC) not to go out to a particular battle. The emperor disregarded the advice and dismissed the general instead. The general became so frustrated that he committed suicide by jumping into a river. Since he was very popular with the citizens, they made rice-dumplings stuffed with meat and threw them into the river in the hope that the fish would eat them instead of the corpse of the general. Meanwhile, some of them went in boats to fish out the corpse. To this day, dragon-boat races are held during this festival. The original dumplings were made by stuffing rice and meat into short lengths of bamboo tubes and then boiling them. With time, bamboo leaves were used instead of bamboo stems to wrap the rice-dumplings which, today, are eaten and enjoyed by the Chinese once a year.

6. 7th month, 15th day: Hungry Ghost Festival (饿鬼节) **or Zhong Yuan Jie** (中元节)
Ghosts, which are the disembodied souls of dead people, are released from hell during the seventh month to roam the earth. Chinese people burn incense and joss-papers, and offer food and tea on road-

sides to appease the ghosts.

7. 8th month, 15th day: Moon-cake or Mid-autumn Festival (中秋节)

This was an ancient harvest festival, to which were attached many myths and legends. One story is that the Chinese wanted to overthrow the Mongols who were ruling China during the Yuan dynasty (1271-1368). The fifteenth night of the eighth month, when there would be a full moon in the sky, was arranged to be the time when all Chinese were to rise up against the Mongols. Messages were baked into cakes and handed out to all Chinese families. This insurrection resulted in the overthrow of the Mongols and culminated in the rise of the Ming Dynasty. The insurgents waved lanterns from hilltop to hilltop to signal to one another their success. This explains why moon-cakes are eaten during this festival and lanterns are carried about by children at night.

Another story says that there were originally nine (some accounts say ten) suns in the sky and they took turns to come out. On one particular occasion, all nine of them came out at the same time causing widespread draught and famine. A man by the name of Hou Yi (后羿) used his magic bow and arrows to shoot down eight of the suns. The remaining sun transformed itself into a man and came down to earth to avenge the death of his eight brother-suns. Hou Yi was not in and his beautiful wife Chang'e (嫦娥) (pronounced Chang Er) was in a strait to escape the wrath of the sun-man. She finally ate a magic herb that her husband had kept in a box. The herb was supposed to have the power to make a person immortal. After eating the herb, Chang'e felt herself becoming lighter and lighter until she gradually floated and rose to the moon. Chinese people pray to the moon because the immortalised Chang'e is there.

8. 9th month, 9th day: Birthday of the Nine-Emperor-Gods (九皇爷)

These gods are said to be the sons of the Goddess of the North Star, Dou Mu (斗母) who keeps the record of life and death. Celebration often starts on the first day of the month. On the ninth night of the month, the idol representing this god is carried round the town with a large procession of people following behind. Mediums run wildly in a trance as they follow the procession. The people carry banners and burn incense. It is believed that the gods are able to give happiness, prosperity, and longevity.

9. 11th month: Winter Solstice Festival (冬至)

The date of this festival varies each year. Its origin can be traced back to the Yin Yang philosophy of Daoism. Winter marks the close of another year and one becomes a year older when the New Year comes. The increase in age is celebrated at the beginning of winter by making marble-sized dough from glutinous rice flour and boiled with sugar. The sweet stew is eaten by everyone in the family. The rice-balls denote the years that have passed.

10. 12th month, 24th day: Return of the Gods to Heaven

On this day, the various gods return to heaven to report the behaviour of the different families to the God-of-heaven. Food is offered to send off the gods. A sweetened pudding made from glutinous rice flour is specially offered to the Kitchen-god so that his mouth would be sweetened to give a good report of the family. The gods would return again to earth on the fourth day of the first month and remain for another year.

Chinese festivals may be generally divided into religious and non-religious ones, depending on what they are meant to celebrate. Of those listed above, the even-numbered ones (i.e. 2, 4, 6, 8 and 10) are religious while the rest are non-religious.[2] The non-religious ones are either obviously based on folklore or meant to commemorate some historical events. The Chinese Religion has diffused into nearly all areas of Chinese life such that even the non-religious festivals are often celebrated by offering food to idols. Noting the different intentions of these festivals, however, help us to determine what are permissible and what are forbidden to Christians.

Christians are forbidden to participate in any of the religious festivals for the same three reasons as they are forbidden to eat food

---

[2]These are the main festivals. Different dialect groups celebrate other festivals peculiar to themselves, while some festivals are preserved in some parts of the world and not in other parts, due to political or practical reasons. An example is the Wangkang festival celebrated occasionally by the Fujian-speaking people of Melaka, Malaysia. Another is the annual Chingay Parade (真艺or 妆艺) seen in Penang, Johor Bahru and Singapore, which has evolved to become a multi-cultural show.

offered to idols. The three reasons are: (i) religious festivals have to do with demons and Christians are forbidden by God to associate with them; (ii) Christians must preserve a clear witness to the non-Christian world by not associating themselves with the Chinese Religion; and (iii) Christians must not cause weaker brethren to stumble by their participation in the festivals.

When a religious festival is celebrated in a temple, it is obvious that the Christian should not go there (1 Cor. 8:10). When the celebration is in the home, the Christian may face with some difficulties. Non-participation means that he does not help in cutting the red paper frills used for decorating the offered food and the altar table, neither does he help out in folding the joss-papers ready for burning. However, the Christian may help out in preparing the food since a portion of it is going to be set aside for himself while the bigger portion is offered to the idols. In this case, the Christian is helping out not because he wishes to participate in celebrating the festival but because he wishes to help in preparing the food that he and his family are going to eat. In short, the Christian must not be seen to participate in, or be supportive of, the religious festivals as far as possible. This often means that the Christian is going to be the odd one out in the family. However, the price of this short period of awkwardness is nothing compared to what happened to the Lord Jesus Christ on the cross.

As for the non-religious festivals, the Christian may quite safely participate in them without getting involved in the religious rites. The religious rites are often kept low-keyed and simple compared to the more elaborate ones during the religious festivals. The Christian may freely enjoy Chinese New Year, exchange moon-cakes with friends and enjoy eating rice-dumplings and rice-ball stew that have not been offered to the idols.

Questions

1 Ah Kow is a Christian. His parents are preparing to celebrate a religious festival at home. Should he help in: (a) folding the joss-papers ready for burning; (b) preparing the food, most of which are going to be offered to idols?

2 Should Christians celebrate the non-religious festivals in order to make use of them in evangelising their non-Christian friends?

3 What would you say to a Christian who collects idols as a hobby? Is his peculiar taste a reflection of a perverse character, and even an unregenerate heart? What if he is an anthropologist or archaeologist by profession/training?

References

1 Chingay Parade in Singapore. 2019. https://www.youtube.com/watch?v=y-Q2va_dKfA (Last accessed, March 2020.)

2 The Wangkang festival, description: https://www.thestar.com.my/lifestyle/star2.com-video/2018/03/03/wangkang (Last accessed, March 2020.)

3 The Wangkang festival, video recording: https://www.thestartv.com/v/wangkang-in-melaka (Last accessed, March 2020.)

Seven

WORSHIPPING THE DEAD (1 Sam. 28:1-25)

Many Christians are blissfully ignorant of the significance of various rites carried out during a Chinese funeral. When a death occurs in the family of the believer, he is caught off guard and does not know what he should or should not do. There also are times when he has to attend a funeral in the home of a friend or a relative. Then there is the annual All Souls Day when he is faced with the various rites carried out by the family. This chapter is intended to help the Christian on such occasions.

7.1   At A Funeral

During a funeral, the coffin is placed in the main hall if the deceased died at home, or in the front porch if the deceased died while away from home. A Christian attending a funeral in the home of a friend or relative may show his last respect by standing in front of the coffin and bow forward slightly, once. He may help out during the funeral by making the mourners' clothes, arranging the furniture and cooking for those who attend.

He may not burn joss-sticks to the deceased as others do, for this will be tantamount to worshipping the dead. There are those who take advantage of the funeral as licence to gamble, normally by playing mahjong, in the house of the bereaved family. The Christian should not participate in, nor encourage, this. It has become an accepted custom among many rural Chinese, but it is really a mockery to gamble during a bereavement.

In a rich family, professional mourners are sometimes employed to mourn. The professional mourners do not weep out of sympathy or love for the bereaved family nor for the deceased, which otherwise would be quite permissible (Rom. 12:15; John 11:35-36). Theirs is a false wailing which is carried out for the money. This is not a good custom as mourning should be done by the bereaved only if it is to be genuine. Scripture is against hypocrisy. The Lord Jesus Christ constantly rebuked hypocrites (Matt. 23:13, 28; 24:51). It is commanded in the Bible that Christians are to lay aside all hypocrisies (1 Pet. 2:1).

When there is a death in his own family, the Christian would naturally be grieved and he should feel free to mourn accordingly. In this case, the mourning is not forced and there is no pretence. The Scriptures are full of examples of godly men who mourned. Abraham mourned for Sarah (Gen. 23:2), Jacob for Joseph (Gen, 37:34-36), the Israelites for Moses (Deut. 34:8), David for Saul and Jonathan (2 Sam. 1:11-27), and the disciples for Jesus (Mark 16:10). The Christian may sit (but not kneel) with the other mourners in the family by the side of the coffin, as required by Chinese custom. It is permissible for the Christian to wear the mourner's clothes and cap (cf. Gen. 37:34). In a Chinese family, the colour of the mourner's apparel depends upon the generation. With most dialect groups, the mourner wears white, or sometimes black, if the deceased is his parent. He wears navy blue if the deceased is his grandparent. The colour is light green if the deceased is his great-grandparent. Some dialect groups wear black for all generations. Needless to say, a Christian should make sure that he wears proper clothing of the correct colour.

An elaborate ceremony is conducted by Buddhist or Taoist monks during the funeral in which all the mourners are expected to participate. This is a religious rite during which the soul of the deceased is supposed to be led through its journey into the spirit-world. The Christian may not participate in this ceremony. When the cortege leaves for the cemetery, the Christian may accompany it. He should not kneel and burn joss-sticks or clasp his palms together in worship after the coffin has been lowered into the grave. He may, however, throw a lump of earth over the coffin as others do, before the grave is covered up, as a gesture of a last service performed to the deceased.

The various things that the Christian abstains from should not necessarily cause any ill-feeling in the family if his stand has already been explained to them before hand. His love for the deceased before he died should not be questionable. It would help if the pastor of his church or a mature Christian friend is present during the funeral to lend him moral support. Moreover, it may not be possible for the Christian to remember the many do's and don'ts when he is already bereaved. The pastor or Christian friend would be of tremendous help if he is present to quietly point these out to him.

It may be that despite all prior explanations, the family still insists on the Christian joining the various ceremonies when the times arrive. The pressure may be intense when the family stands under the scrutiny of relatives who consider it utterly unfilial not to join in the ceremonies. It is not for us to criticise or condemn a brother who is forced to comply. The Lord knows that his heart is not in what he is forced to do. If anything, such a brother needs our love and understanding all the more. We do well to remember that Elisha did not condemn Naaman but said instead, "Go in peace", when he was forced to constantly bow before false gods (2 Kings 5:15-19). The Christian, however, is urged to stand firm in the faith under such pressures. "Rejoice to the extent that you partake of Christ's sufferings, that when His glory is revealed, you may also be glad with exceeding joy" (1 Pet. 4:13). The day will come when "God will wipe away every tear from your eyes" (Rev. 7:17; 21:4, 7).

7.2   Qingming Jie (清明节) or All Souls Day

We have classified this as a religious festival because of its obvious connection with ancestral worship. The Bible makes it plain that no contact is possible between the living and the souls of the dead. Any attempt to do so is sinful. Food that is offered to ancestors will never reach them. Moreover, this practice is forbidden by God (Deut. 26:14). Bowing to them in worship is also sinful.

Luke 16:31 says that, "If they do not hear Moses and the Prophets; neither will they be persuaded though one rise from the dead." The words used indicate that the rising of the dead is only hypothetical. The dead will not rise except on the last day, though the Lord has the power to raise them at any time (cf. 1 Cor. 15:50-53). The incident recorded in Matthew 27:52 when "the graves were opened; and many bodies of the saints, who had fallen asleep were raised" occurred in direct connection with the death and resurrection of Jesus Christ, and is not intended to be a norm. Just as Lazarus had earlier been raised by the Lord, these believers were raised to emphasise the fact that Jesus Christ is "the resurrection and the life" (John 11:25). After all, man is destined to die once, and after that to face the judgement (Heb. 9:27).

Our main interest here is not to consider whether the dead will rise but to establish the fact that there is no possibility of contact between the living and the souls of the dead. From Luke 16:19-31 (the incident of the Rich Man and Lazarus) we learn that there is no possibility for the souls of the dead to contact the living, and we would expect the reverse to be true as well. The incident of Saul consulting the spirit of Samuel (1 Sam. 28) is often quoted in support of the possibility of such contact. Careful study of the passage, however, reveals that it was not Samuel's spirit that was raised but it was Satan who impersonated the spirit of Samuel. We advance five reasons for saying so.[1]

i God had just refused to answer Saul by the (then) normal means of dreams, Urim or prophets (v. 6). It is inconceivable that He will now answer Saul by a method which is detestable and condemned (Deut. 18:11).

ii It must have been an evil spirit that appeared because he received the worship of Saul (v. 14). Good spirits will never receive worship from any man (cf. Rev. 19:10; 22:8, 9).

iii The true Samuel, who was so zealous for God, and so faithful a reprover, would have reproved Saul for consulting the dead.

iv No evil spirit, not even Satan, has the power to disturb the soul of a believer who has returned to God (Eccles. 12:7), who has entered into peace and found rest (Isaiah 57:2), who is at Abraham's bosom (Luke 16:22), and who has rested from his labour (Rev. 14:13).

v It is recorded that Saul died because he was unfaithful to the Lord, one of his sins being that he consulted a medium for guidance (1 Chron. 10:13).

[1]See Matthew Poole's Commentary.

It is clear that no contact is possible between the living and the dead. Note, however, that remembrance for the dead is different from worshipping them. Remembrance for them is not sinful. A monument may be built to the remembrance of the brave soldiers who sacrificed their lives for the country. A day may be set aside to remember them. The remembrance service may be carried out in different ways. Flowers may be placed at the monument, trumpets may be blown and a minute's silence may be observed. All these are done as gestures and not because we expect the dead to be able to appreciate them.

Similarly, it would be quite permissible for the Christian to go to the cemetery with the family on All Souls Day and help to clear the tomb off weeds. In practice, however, this is going to be difficult because the Christian would have to observe the rest of the family offering food, burning incense and joss-papers, and kneeling in prayer. Besides, there is a small stone tablet by the side of the tomb before which joss-sticks are burnt to the God-of-the-earth. So, spirit worship is also involved. Moreover, he would be the odd one out if he does not participate by helping to carry the baskets of food up and down the hill where the cemetery is normally located. We note that those living in big cities are increasingly having the dead buried in well-kept burial parks operated by corporate companies, where the hassle of cleaning the tomb is taken out of the hands of the family. The basic procedures of worship, however, remain the same.

It is suggested, therefore, that the Christian should explain to the parents his dilemma and ask to be allowed to stay at home where he can pray to God, giving thanks for every remembrance of the deceased and asking for God's blessings to be upon the family. The dead must not be prayed for, neither must they be prayed to. It may help to visit other Christian friends or have them come to your home on that day so that you can pray and have fellowship together. During an occasion like this, we should pray for the salvation of those in our families. We should yearn more for their salvation than for the opportunity to go to the cemetery to see them pray to the dead.

An alternative day has been suggested for Christians to visit the graves of the deceased, such as on Easter day, or on a day during the Chinese New Year. Formidable problems are involved because: (i) time must be taken off work if it is not a public holiday; (ii) not all family members might place importance on visiting the grave; (iii) unconverted family members are made to feel awkward to be reminded of death and the deceased, especially on a happy occasion such as the Chinese New Year. The suggestion of an alternative day is certainly not practical for first-generation Christians. However, when one is married and living separately from the parents – as is often the case – the Christian family may quietly visit the grave of the deceased on the eve of the Chinese New Year. There is no necessity of announcing it to the extended family, nor is there any need to hide it from them when they find out. This has been our practice ever since my father passed away. Our immediate family would gather together before the grave to take a photograph, after which we would pray to God. We would give thanks to God as we remember the deceased, pray for the salvation of unconverted family members, and commit our lives to Him. We would then drive on to join the extended family for the reunion dinner. An annual visit to the grave to remember the dead has had a sobering effect on our lives – making us see life in the perspective of eternity, stirring up gratitude for our salvation, and drawing us near to God.

7.3   Three Helpful Rules

The Chinese culture is full of festivals and it is impossible to discuss everyone of them in detail. Moreover, various dialect groups celebrate them in different ways and this makes it difficult to state what activities are permissible and what are forbidden to Christians. We shall attempt, however, to give three general rules by which a Christian may check whether an activity is permissible to him or not.

I claim no credit in formulating these rules. I have learnt them from others and found them helpful. It is hoped that other people will find them helpful, too.[2] Here they are: A Christian may do everything provided,

i it does not break God's Law;

ii it does not hinder his own spiritual progress; and

iii it does not cause harm to others, especially to fellow-Christians.

---

[2]*P.S.* A positive way of stating it, based on 2 Chron. 31:20-21, is: (i) determine what is right and good and true before God (i.e. from the Scripture); (ii) do it with all your heart; (iii) trust God to prosper you.

It can be seen that in order not to break God's law, it is necessary to have a knowledge of His law. The law of God referred to here is all-encompassing. It includes the Ten Commandments in particular (Ex. 20:1-7; Deut. 5:6-21), and all the other principles which are either stated in, or clearly deducible from, the Bible. A number of such principles have been applied to various situations in this, and the previous, chapters. A Christian is not expected to know all that there is to know within a short span of time. However, it is incumbent upon him to study the Scripture diligently and in dependence upon the Holy Spirit to give understanding.

It can also be seen that these rules are based on the scriptural teaching that "All things are lawful for me, but all things are not helpful; all things are lawful for me, but all things do not edify" (1 Cor. 10:23). If the Christian is troubled at any time because he is not sure whether a particular activity is permissible to him, he should refrain. "Whatever is not from faith (i.e. conviction) is sin" (Rom. 14:23).

We should note, however, that our lives are not to be controlled by the scruples of others. There is a class of people who are weak in conscience and strong at wanting to impose their scruples upon others. 1 Corinthians 10:23 is no licence for such people to try to enslave others. 'If you died with Christ from the basic principles of the world, why, as though living in the world, do you subject yourselves to regulations – "Do not touch, do not taste, do not handle...?"' (Col. 2:20-21).

Questions

1 The Early Church split over the question of whether to allow those Christians who succumbed to the pressure of idol (emperor) worship to come back into communion with the church. When a Christian succumbs under pressure to burn incense to idols, what should the church do to him? Why?

2 When a Christian's own father or mother has passed away, it may be difficult for him to stay at home instead of going with the family to the cemetery on All Souls Day. What would you suggest that he do?

3 Should Christians visit their friends and eat in their homes during

a holy day such as *Deepavali* and *Hari Raya Haji*? (cf. Gal. 4:10; Rom. 14:5).

4 "But I do not want you to be ignorant, brethren, concerning those who have fallen asleep, lest you sorrow as others who have no hope. For if we believe that Jesus died and rose again, even so God will bring with Him those who sleep in Jesus" (1 Thess. 4:13-14). Is there any difference between mourning and grieving (sorrow)? What should our reaction be if the deceased were: (a) an unbeliever; (b) a believer? Why?

Reference

1 Matthew Poole's Commentary on the Holy Bible. MacDonald.

Eight

TWO MISTAKES TO AVOID (1 Thess. 5:12-22)

There are two mistakes which a Chinese Christian is prone to make. The first mistake is to have an over negative attitude towards the Chinese culture. The other is to transport the mystical atmosphere of the Chinese Religion into his Christian life. The first of these is treated briefly here, while more space is devoted to the second.

There are occasions when we need not fear being labelled 'over-negative'. It is the bane of modern Evangelicalism to hear so few voices raised to warn against errors and heresies in the church. Too many people are fearful of being labelled 'negative'. So many are afraid of being charged with 'quenching the Holy Spirit', 'lacking love', and so on. Indeed, there are times when it is necessary to be negative in order to be positive because of being faithful to God's word. On the other hand, there is the danger of Christians being over-negative towards things that are in themselves innocent and when no biblical principles are compromised. An over-negative attitude towards the Chinese culture is certainly something to be avoided.

The second mistake the Chinese Christian is prone to make has to do with the Charismatic movement. Much has been written about this movement (Masters and Whitcomb, 2016; Butler, 1985). One respected author has shown that the birth and growth of the movement may be traced to the prevailing general atmosphere of the world today (Hulse, 1977). The factors that contribute to this ideal atmosphere include the aftermath of the Second World War, the Cold War, the failures of secular humanistic philosophies, of the drug and pop-music culture, and the deadness of nominal Christianity. From the 1960's, the Charismatic movement has spread like wild fire in Asia. One important contributory factor for this, which should not be overlooked, is the mysticism that is inherent in the cultures of Asia. The beliefs and practices of the Charismatic movement are readily welcomed by a people whose outlook is already influenced by the mysticism of the eastern religions, including that of the Chinese Religion.

8.1   An Over-negative Attitude

We have examined the Chinese Religion and denounced it for what it is. However, there are many aspects of the Chinese culture that are harmless, except for the tinge of religion that tends to colour everything Chinese. If this tinge of religion is removed, it would be seen that these aspects of culture are beautiful and rich in aesthetic value.

Chinese painting, calligraphy, literature and poems are the invaluable heritage of the Chinese people and should not be lightly dismissed as worthless or irrelevant. The lion dance that is performed during Chinese New Year often involves praying to ancestral altars. When performed during, say, the National Day of a country, no such ancestral worship is observed. On such an occasion, when no ancestral worship is even hinted to, there is no reason why a Christian may not engage in it. Chinese *gongfu* is too often condemned because of the violence that is associated with it. The violence has been grossly exaggerated by the movies. Violence is unavoidable under certain circumstances, as when soldiers have to defend the country against attacks by foreign enemies. A Christian who joins the army is doing an honourable job (cf. Luke 7:1-10 and Acts 10 where the centurions were not asked to forsake their profession), and unarmed combat is just part of his training. *Gongfu* has been perfected through the many centuries of Chinese history and is now taught to soldiers in many countries, including The People's Republic of China and the United States of America. Those who have some knowledge of the art will be able to appreciate it as a superb art form. It can be taught and practised without involving any form of religious rites. No doubt many novices tend to show off their abilities but, as in any sphere of achievement, time soon robs it off its novelty. We suggest that it is up to the individual Christian to judge whether he may practise the art or not.

Many Chinese customs, too, are harmless though some of them may seem silly in our time. An older relative is greeted by calling him or her "Uncle" or "Auntie". Before a meal, it is polite for the children to ask their parents to eat. When visiting friends or relatives, especially older folk, it is good to bring along some cakes or fruits. One should bring along only an even number of fruits, say, four or six. When drink is served, it is polite to ask the host or hostess to drink before one starts drinking. It is also polite for the guest not to completely finish the drink, but to leave some of it at the bottom of the cup. Before leaving, we should inform the older folk in the house. The *hongbao* given during Chinese New Year or on other occasions should contain money totalling to an even number, e.g. two dollars, six dollars or ten dollars, and not five dollars or fifteen dollars. This is not adhered to by some who are either ignorant or apathetic.

The over-negative attitude of some Chinese Christians to the Chinese culture has not helped them in the evangelisation of their compatriots. Ignorance of the Chinese customs on the part of Christians has caused many unconverted Chinese to comment on how 'westernised' and 'uncultured' the Christians are. Beware of the over-negative attitude!

8.2 Mysticism

By mysticism we do not mean here the sense of rapture and ecstasy that a Christian may experience when he meditates upon, and is absorbed with, the things of God. The apostle Paul seemed to have been caught up into such ecstasy on several occasions when he burst into praise and glory for the Lord (2 Cor. 12:1-5; Eph. 1:3-14; 3; Col. 1:10-20). The apostle John was similarly caught up in ecstasy when he was on the Isle of Patmos (Rev. 1:9ff.). A. W. Tozer considered certain past church leaders and hymn writers, like John Newton, Charles Wesley and F. W. Faber, to be mystics (Tozer, 1963). We may note three points that are characteristic of the experiences of these men:

  i their experiences were rooted in, and flowed from, a deep knowledge of God's Word;

  ii God alone was seen to be greatly magnified, and there was no
trace of self-glorification;

  iii their experiences resulted in some positive work being accomplished for God. In the case of the apostles, the will of God was
revealed. In the case of those whom Tozer called mystics, the
gospel was preached and hymns were written.

What we wish to discuss here is the mysticism akin to that found
in the Chinese Religion. It is characterised by a sense of wonder at
the miraculous, a fear of the unknown and the presence of a tinge
of superstition. It tends to encourage a form of spirituality which
is introspective and divorced from the harsh realities of life. It also
has the effect of turning the attention of believers away from the
objective truths on which Christianity is founded.

The Son of God did become man in the person of Jesus Christ.
The Lord Jesus Christ did die on the cross of Calvary during the time
of the Roman Empire. He did rise from the dead. He did ascend to
heaven and is now interceding for believers. The incarnation, death,
resurrection and ascension of our Lord are not just ideas that were
conjured up by Christians in ages past. They are objective truths.
Faith in and of itself is largely subjective; but in Christianity, it means
personal committal to the person of Christ and what He has done,
and is doing, for the believer. The subjective aspect of faith is, therefore, rooted in the objective facts of the person and work of Christ.
Again, assurance may be largely subjective but for the Christian, the
assurance of his salvation is rooted in these objective truths.

Most, though not all, people who teach or practise the form of
mysticism we are discussing here are suggestible and excitable personalities. What can be experienced is real and right to them. Often,
the experiences are not rooted in, nor flow from, a deep knowledge
of Scripture, though Bible verses are sometimes quoted to support
the experiences. A Christian who is familiar with the mystical aura
and superstition in the Chinese society may fall victim to such wrong
teachings if he is not careful. Some such wrong teachings are described below.

A Two-tier Christianity
The teaching is that there are two types of Christians. The first type are those who have undergone water baptism but not the baptism of the Spirit. The second type are those who have undergone both baptisms. This teaching implies that the second type of Christians are somehow better and more spiritual than the first. Some even go to the extent of saying that if you do not 'speak in tongues' to prove that you have been baptised in/by the Spirit, you are not a Christian. This teaching has the effect of undermining the assurance of young converts and make them yearn for some mystical experience of the Holy Spirit which would make them speak in unknown tongues.

The Scripture never teaches that speaking in unknown tongues is the proof of one's spirituality, neither is it a proof of whether a person is a Christian or not (1 Cor. 13). This two-tier, Christianity-plus theology cannot be borne out by the Scripture. When you become a Christian, you have the Holy Spirit dwelling in you. You cannot have a portion only of the Spirit. You either have the whole of the Holy Spirit or you have none. You are either a Christian or you are not (Rom. 8:9-17; 1 Cor. 12:13). You become a Christian by exercising faith in Jesus Christ. Jesus Christ has accomplished all that is necessary to secure your salvation (Eph. 2:4-10). Nothing more is necessary, and nothing less is sufficient to save us. Every believer has the Holy Spirit in him. He is, therefore, accepted as a child of God and has access to all that is available from God in Christ (Eph. 1:13-14; Rom. 8:14-17).

The incidents recorded in the second, eighth, tenth and nineteenth chapters of Acts, which the Charismatics often appeal to, are not meant to be normative. In other words, these events are not meant to be examples of the normal experience of Christians today. The incidents recorded in the first three passages show the pouring out of the Spirit for the first time upon the Church, which is made up of Jews (Acts 2), Samaritans (Acts 8) and Gentiles (Acts 10). See Acts 1:8 for confirmation of this. Acts 19 records the conversion of some followers of John the Baptist.

To Be Slain By The Spirit
This teaching has been circulating in Asian churches and the phenomenon of being 'slain by the Spirit' is attributed to the activity of the Holy Spirit. It is seen less today compared to the 1970's and the 1980's. The Chinese Christian must beware of it, however. A

minister or evangelist who is praying in the pulpit may cause one or more persons in the congregation to be thrown down to the ground suddenly. Or, he may call upon individuals to come on stage and touch them to cause them to fall down. Those thrown down are said to have been 'slain by the Spirit' because of harbouring some unconfessed sins. They would recover from the state of shock after the minister or evangelist has laid hand on them and prayed.

Such teaching is not found anywhere in the Scripture. The phenomenon has never been observed throughout church history until in recent years.[1] The teaching may have been based on the incident recorded in Acts 5:1-11 where Ananias and Sapphira were struck dead by God for lying with the intention of showing themselves generous and spiritual. We may note at least three differences between this incident and the present-day phenomenon:

i The apostle Peter did not suggest to the Christians in advance what might happen to them if they lied. Ananias and Sapphira had not seen anyone struck dead instantaneously for lying before. Modern-day preachers suggest to the congregation in advance what may happen to them if they are not truthful. If no suggestions are given by the preachers personally during meetings, their reputation for causing people to be 'slain by the Spirit' is already known.

ii The apostle Peter was given revelation regarding the specific sin of Ananias and Sapphira and he voiced it out to them. Modern-day preachers just make some general remarks over the heads of the congregation about their hidden sins.

iii Ananias and Sapphira died, showing that it was God's judgement on them. Those who are 'slain by the Spirit' today always recover.

The incident in Acts occurred during the transition period when the Church was assuming the structure that God has planned for in preparation for the passing away of the apostles. The local church structure with its elders and deacons is seen to have taken shape nearing the end of the book of Acts (Acts 20:17ff.) and in the epistles of Paul (e.g. 1 Tim. 3; Titus 1:5ff.; Eph. 4:11). This was also the

---

[1]It is not correct to claim that this phenomenon is similar to what is known to have occurred during the revivals of the past. Those emotional frenzy were much more dramatic and much more widespread, but it is equally dubious that they were the work of God. See, for example, Dallimore, vol. 1, 1979.

period when the Scripture was not yet completed and the miracles performed by the apostles were God's way of authenticating their teachings (Acts 14:3; Rom. 15:18, 19; 2 Cor. 12:12; Gal. 3:5; Heb. 2:1-4). No more apostles of the stature of Paul and the Twelve exist today and the canon of Scripture is closed. All that God wanted written down as scriptures are already complete in the Bible. We do not expect there to be signs and wonders everywhere today performed by self-styled 'miracle-workers'.

Healing And Exorcism

Yet another widespread practice in certain Asian churches is healing and casting out demons from individuals. So-called 'deliverance meetings' are held where people are supposedly healed by the laying on of hands and prayers, and demons are cast out.

We believe in the immutability of God and we recognise that the Lord is the same yesterday and today and forever (Heb. 13:8). We also believe that demons are real and the evil one is at work in this world. God can work the miracles that He worked in the past, and He can heal miraculously when His people pray earnestly for healing. However, God's *ability* must not to be confused with God's *purpose*. God is still able to perform the miracles that He performed in the past, but it may not be His purpose to perform them today. God is still able to heal, but this is dependent on His sovereign will. Similarly, demons can be cast out by the power of God "in the name of Jesus Christ". In many 'deliverance meetings', however, we wonder whether the ailments were really there in the first place, and whether the Christians were truly possessed. In one such meeting which I attended, the ailments cured were headaches and stomachaches!

The phrase "in the name of Jesus Christ" has been widely misunderstood and much abused. It does not mean that the name "Jesus Christ" has some magical quality about it that demons fear. Rather, the phrase means, simply, all that is implied in the person and ministry of the Lord Jesus Christ. For example, when Peter healed the crippled man "in the name of Jesus Christ" (Acts 3:6), he meant, "relying on who Jesus Christ is and what He has done (and is doing, interceding for us in heaven)". It is in this sense that there is power and authority in Jesus Christ's name. After the healing, Peter began to preach the gospel (Acts 3:11-26) to amplify on this act (cf. Acts 3:12). In practical terms, therefore, it means that it is through the preaching and hearing of the gospel that demons can be permanently cast out and healing can be effected.

The scriptural teaching is that the healing of the total man is accomplished when the individual turns to the Lord Jesus Christ to be saved. This does not mean that a physical handicap such as a decayed tooth or an amputated arm would be restored to normal again. (It is worth noting that no faith healer has ever been seen healing such handicaps.) Rather, it means that the individual's relationship with God, which was broken at the fall of Adam, is restored. This is a spiritual healing which brings about many emotional as well as physical healings. Many emotional and physical sicknesses are caused by sin in men. Physical death itself is a result of sin. The whole universe is decaying because of the curse of God upon it when the first man, Adam, rebelled against Him (Gen. 3:14-24; Rom. 8:19-22; Col. 1:19-20). The problem of man is a spiritual one. The gospel is, therefore, to be preached so that bruised and broken men may be healed. The apostle Peter himself confirmed this understanding of the healing ministry when he applied the verse in Isaiah 53:5 to the salvation of mankind. "Christ Himself bore our sins in His own body on the tree, that we, having died to sins, might live for righteousness – by whose stripes you were healed" (1 Pet. 2:24).

As for demon possession, we cannot find in the Bible any case of a child of God who is possessed. The reverse is often the case; demon-possessed persons have the demons cast out of them and they become Christians (e.g. Mark 5:18-20; Luke 8:1-3). In Luke 11:24-28, the Lord Jesus Christ explains that when an evil spirit is cast out of a person, the person becomes clean and empty. The evil spirit will return again and enter the same person with seven other evil spirits more wicked than itself. The final condition of that man becomes worse than the first. The lesson is that the person from whom an evil spirit has been cast out should be filled with the Holy Spirit in order to prevent re-entry of other spirits. The Holy Spirit can indwell the person only when the person yields his life to Jesus Christ. He can yield his life to Jesus Christ only when he hears and understands the gospel. Christians are, therefore, to preach the gospel and not to go around seeking for demon-possessed persons from whom they can cast out the demons. The Holy Spirit indwelling the Christian will never allow any evil spirit to enter him. "Do you not know that your body is the temple of the Holy Spirit who is in you?" (1 Cor. 6:19). "He who is in you is greater than he who is in the world" (1 John 4:4).

We suggest the following reasons why so many Christians have demons cast out of them during 'deliverance meetings':

i they are not Christians but may have been misled into thinking that they were;

ii they are Christians but they are not truly demon-possessed. Their conditions are psychologically induced;

iii God may allow evil spirits to temporarily oppress Christians.

"Oppression" may be regarded as a general term that covers "afflictions" (Gk. *thlipsis* or *pathema*) whether physical, mental or spiritual, and "demon possession" (Gk. *daimonizomai*). While Christians cannot be possessed, they may be afflicted. In Acts 10:38, the phrase "oppressed by the devil" is correctly translated "under the power of the devil" in the N.I.V. The original Greek word *katadunasteuo* which is translated "oppressed" means "to exercise dominion against". An example of a believer who was afflicted by Satan is Job who lost his property and family, and contracted sores over his body, all of which were caused by Satan (Job 1:6–12; 2:1-6). Another example of physical affliction by Satan is recorded in Luke 13:10-17. The devout woman was described by our Lord as "a daughter of Abraham" and attending the place of worship. While not demon-possessed, her suffering had been imposed on her by an evil spirit. Also, a believer may be unwittingly used by Satan. Examples are David who was incited by Satan to trust in Israel's strength by taking a census instead of trusting in God (1 Chron. 21:1 cf. 2 Sam. 24:1), and Peter who was unwittingly used by Satan to prevent the Lord from going to the cross (Luke 22:31; Matt. 16:23; Mark 8:33 cf. Luke 4:13; Matt. 4:10). Believers may be oppressed by the devil only with the expressed permission of God. Healing those who are oppressed is part of our Lord's ministry (Acts 10:38).

It is my belief that many preachers/healers in 'deliverance meetings' are wilfully exploiting the emotions and suggestible nature of the congregations, or they sincerely believe, but are sincerely wrong, in what they practise. It is deceitful of preachers to exploit the emotions and suggestible natures of others.

Spirit-infused Objects
We consider one final example of mysticism which Christians may

fall into. This is to attach particular importance to objects, pictures and symbols. Some people have been known to keep crucifixes in the house for the sole purpose of warding off evil. This is similar to the Chinese practice of hanging the dried shoulder blades of pigs on the lintel of every doorway leading into the house to ward off evil spirits. This is nothing more than superstition.

Others would have nothing to do with pictures of temples and mosques because they consider them to be 'spirit-infused'. They would also have nothing to do with pictures of dragons because of their connection with the mythical Chinese god, the Dragon-god-of-the-sea. If this teaching is carried through to its logical conclusion, it would not be possible for a Christian to stay on in his home since there are idols in it which his family worship.

Yet others would seek guidance from God by opening the Bible arbitrarily and taking the first verse that the eyes fall upon as the words of God for them. The Bible is thus treated like a book of omens.[2]

All these fall short of the New Testament teaching of what is true religion. The New Testament emphasises the inwardness and spiritual character of true religion. "The kingdom of God is not food and drink, but righteousness and peace and joy in the Holy Spirit" (Rom. 14:17). "My kingdom is not of this world" (John 18:36). "The kingdom of God is within you" (Luke 17:21). "God is Spirit, and those who worship Him must worship in spirit and truth" (John 4:24). "In Christ Jesus neither circumcision nor uncircumcision avails anything, but faith working through love" (Gal. 5:6). "Neither circumcision nor uncircumcision avails anything, but a new creation" (Gal. 6:15). Christians must no longer place undue importance on objects, pictures or symbols. Even if these are used in occult practices against Christians, God will never allow any evil force to harm His people (Num. 23:23; I John 5:18-19).

8.3   Some Concluding Remarks

There seems to be an inappropriate interest among some Christians in Asia on the subject of demonology. In many cases there is an inadequate, or a total lack of, teaching on this subject. As a result,

---

[2]See (Ferguson, 1984; Sproul, 1984; Masters, 2008) for helpful books on seeking God's guidance.

Christians are only too ready to imbibe the first teaching on the subject from any speaker. We wish to caution the reader to "take heed how you hear" (Luke 8:18) because a lot of dubious teachings are being propagated. 'Not everyone who says to Me, "Lord, Lord," shall enter the kingdom of heaven, but he who does the will of My Father in heaven. Many will say to Me on that day, "Lord, Lord, have we not prophesied in Your name, cast out demons in Your name, and done many wonders in Your name?" And then I will declare to them, "I never knew you; depart from Me, you who practise lawlessness!"' (Matt. 7:21-23). It is amazing to find Christians inordinately absorbed with the devil and his activities. It is God whom we should fear, not Satan.[3]

There is also an inordinate absorption with the person and activity of the Holy Spirit. We would hold suspect any individual or group of people who talk too much about the Holy Spirit. Men who are constantly living under the conscious guidance of the Holy Spirit see no need for repeated mention of the Holy Spirit. The function of the Holy Spirit is to glorify the Lord Jesus Christ (John 15:26; 16:14, 15), and we expect Christians to focus their attention more on the Lord Jesus Christ than on the Holy Spirit. This is not to say that we are to be silent about the person and work of the Holy Spirit. The right teachings about the Holy Spirit must be given so that Christians would not be open to the spurious teachings we hear so much of today.

It is interesting to note that many teachings and practices in Asian churches come from the West like fashions of dress. At one time the 'mini-skirt' was popular in the West. It became popular in Asia at the time when it was going out of popularity in the West. The 'maxi' then came into fashion. A little later, when the popularity was waning in the West, it became popular in Asia. Similarly, when the advance of the so-called 'Charismatic movement' began to plateau off in the West, it caught on in the East. Healing and exorcism, which was a hot topic in the West, has spread to the East. The East, however, is not devoid of originality. When the type of mysticism we have discussed in this chapter arrived in Asia, it found the ground congenial for it to flourish. After all, Asia is the home ground of the more obvious forms of religious mysticism. It is not surprising, therefore, to

---

[3]See (Masters, 2016) for a helpful book that examines Charismatic healing and exorcism in the light of the Bible.

find so many unwary Asian Christians succumb to these teachings on extraordinary gifts and experiences and, in fact, introducing new ones themselves.

We need to be clear as to what is the issue at stake. By advocating experience as another rule of faith side by side with Scripture, and often over-riding it, the Charismatic movement is, in fact, trying to destroy the principle of *sola Scriptura* (Scripture only) held by Evangelical Christians from the Reformation and, we dare say, from the apostolic age, until now. By advocating that God still speaks through men in the form of prophecies just as He did in ages past, they are in fact saying that Scripture is insufficient. When the principle of *sola Scriptura* is destroyed, the Church is open to all kinds of error and weird teaching. This was what happened before the Reformation. The Church of Rome maintained (and still maintains) that oral tradition was a necessary complement to the written word. The result was an age in which vital Christianity was wiped out and superstition reigned, until the Reformation came with the recovery of Scripture. It was not only the Church of Rome that had a low opinion of Scripture. Even in the early church some of the mystical sects, such as the Montanists and the Cathari, regarded the Bible as quite superfluous. And in the days of the Reformation a section of the Anabaptists (not to be confused with the Baptists!) and the Libertines of Geneva were of the same opinion. The extreme section of the Anabaptists especially asserted the absolute necessity of the inner light and of all kinds of special revelations. The view of all these groups were never held by the mainstream of Christianity. For example, the early church had a high view of Scripture in contrast to the Montanists and the Cathari. With the passing away of the apostles, and the completion of the Bible, the extraordinary gifts of tongues, prophecies and healing gradually faded away (cf. 1 Cor. 13:8). Therefore, in all the early church councils, it was the Bible that the Christians used to counter heresies and to seek the mind of God on problems the church was facing.

What has the Bible to say about itself? The sufficiency and inspiration of Scripture is stated in the well-known passage of 2 Timothy 3:16-17, "All Scripture is given by inspiration of God, and is profitable for doctrine, for reproof, for correction, for instruction in righteousness, that the man of God may be completed, thoroughly equipped for every good work." Similarly, we find in 2 Peter 1:20-21, "No prophecy of Scripture is of any private interpretation for prophecy never came by the will of man, but holy men of God spoke as they were moved by the Holy Spirit." The apostles were aware that what they taught were the inspired words of God (cf. 1 Thess. 2:13) and what they wrote were Scriptures (cf. 2 Pet. 3:16). Hence, when John wrote the book of Revelation, he must have been aware that he was the last surviving apostle who was writing Scriptures. The words contained in Revelation 22:18-19 must refer to the whole Bible, and not to the book of Revelation only – "I testify to everyone who hears the words of the prophecy of this book: If anyone adds to these things, God will add to him the plagues that are written in this book; and if anyone takes away from the words of the book of this prophecy, God shall take away his part from the Book of Life, from the holy city, and from the things which are written in this book." The Lord Jesus Christ Himself said, "Heaven and earth will pass away, but My words will by no means pass away" (Matt. 24:35). The principle of *sola Scriptura* is based on Scripture itself.

A study of Church history reveals that the devil alternated between attacking the Church from within and from without. It is the ignorant man who says that our enemies lie outside the Church only. Our Lord Himself warned us against enemies who would creep into the Church – "Beware of false prophets, who come to you in sheep's clothing but inwardly they are ravenous wolves" (Matt. 7:15; see also Acts 20:28-31). Various forces are contending for supremacy over the minds of Christians. We do well to heed our Lord's warning.

> You did not receive the spirit of bondage again to fear, but you received the Spirit of adoption (Rom. 8:15). You were bought at a price; do not become slaves of men (1 Cor. 7:23). Stand fast therefore in the liberty by which Christ has made us free, and do not be entangled again with a yoke of bondage (Gal. 5:1).

Questions

1 Chinese-educated Chinese are more polite compared to western-educated Chinese. Do you agree? Why?

2 Judged by our definition of 'mysticism', many Christians appear to have fallen into it. What is the cure?

3 A group of young ladies from the church went to a Christian camp. On returning, they visited their pastor. They saw a picture of a lion on the floor mat and told the pastor that he should destroy the mat because the Bible says "the devil is like a roaring lion". The pastor answered by saying that the Bible also describes the Lord Jesus Christ as "the Lion of the tribe of Judah". The ladies next saw a couple of Chinese lanterns hanging in the hall. They told the pastor that the lanterns should be destroyed because of the dragons on them. The pastor decided not to answer them. When the ladies departed the pastor removed the floor mat and the lanterns for the sake of the conscience of those ladies. What can you say about: (a) those ladies; (b) the pastor?

References

1 Butler, C. S. 1985. Test the Spirits. Evangelical Press.

2 Dallimore, Arnold. 1979. George Whitefield, Vo. 1, Ch. 19. Banner of Truth Trust.

3 Ferguson, Sinclair. 1984. Discovering God's Will. Banner of Truth Trust.

4 Hulse, Erroll. 1977. The Believer's Experience. Carey Pubs.

5 Masters, Peter. 2008. Steps For Guidance. Wakeman Trust.

6 Masters, Peter and Whitcomb, John C. 2016. The Charismatic Illusion. Wakeman Trust.

7 Sproul, R. C. 1984. God's Will and the Christian. Scripture Union.

8 Tozer, A. W. 1963. The Christian Book of Mystical Verses. Christian Pubs. Inc.

Appendix 1: WATARI

In Matthew 12:25-26 we read these words of the Lord Jesus Christ, "Every Kingdom divided against itself is brou-ght to desolation, and every city or house divided against itself will not stand. And if Satan casts our Satan, he is divided against himself How then will his kingdom stand?" Chinese Christians are often perplexed by the apparent enmity between the spirits worshipped by the Chinese people. There are the good spirits and the wicked spirits. A person may employ the help of a wicked spirit that indwells a particular medium to cause affliction on someone else. The family of the person so afflicted may consult a medium who is indwelt by a good, and stronger, spirit to break the charm of the wicked spirit. Based on the Bible verse just quoted, it is assumed not probable that both the good and bad spirits are the agents of Satan.

We know from the Bible that the Spirit of God alone dwells in a person who has come to faith in Christ. There is no indication that angels who serve God dwell in people, regardless of whether they are believers or unbelievers. We do read, however, of evil spirits, or demons, entering men and animals. See for example, Mark 5. It follows that the 'good spirits' and the 'bad spirits' in the demonology of the Chinese must be the agents of Satan. The enmity between them is only apparent, the purpose of which is to make the whole affair seem convincing. The story of Watari may help to illustrate the point.

As a young boy, I saw a Japanese movie entitled *Watari*. The story was about a boy by the name of Watari who was taught the fighting arts of the *Ninjas* by his grandfather. Watari's father and grandfather had been members of a secret society whose leaders hid their identity by wearing masks each time that they met. That secret society was at war with another. Watari's father discovered a secret in his society and was ruthlessly killed as a result. Watari's grandfather barely escaped death himself and lost a leg in the process.

When Watari had finished his training in the fighting arts, he went to seek revenge for the death of his father. He fought his way through the secret society, finally killing the chief. When the mask was removed from the dead man, it was revealed that he had been the chief of both warring secret societies! This one man had been responsible for the plots and counterplots between the two secret societies by wearing different masks, all to further his own ends. This was the secret that Watari's father had discovered and for which he was killed.

Satan is more subtle than many of us think.

Appendix 2: PUKAU

In Malaysia cases of *pukau* have been reported. This is when a person is supposed to have been charmed so that he is not aware of what is done to him after that. Houses have been broken into and thoroughly ransacked without any of the occupants being aware of it until the next morning. Young girls have willingly been taken for rides, ending in their jewellery being stripped off and sometimes being molested.

While not denying the possibility of men using evil forces to further their wicked plans, I suggest that other explanations lie behind these cases. The house-breakers could have burnt the dried leaves of a certain plant (perhaps *ganja* i.e. cannabis?) near the bedroom windows, the smoke of which caused the occupants of the house to become drowsy. It may simply have been that the house-breakers were very efficient in their job and the occupants were too sound asleep, and the story of having been charmed was spread around later to *save face*. After all, there are just as many cases reported of occupants who had awakened and put up a fight with the house-breakers.

There is all the more reason for the young girls who had been taken for rides to *save face*. They should have blamed it on their own gullibility rather than on having been *pukau-ed*. We are not unaware of the various methods of hypnosis (for example, the handshake interrupt method) but these work only on compliant and suggestible personalities.

Appendix 3: BOWING IN THE BIBLE

It is of interest to us to make a more detailed study on bowing in the Bible. This is particularly so because Chinese culture is full of bowing. In olden day China, emperors, army officials, magistrates and petty officers were bowed to by the citizens. Parents were also bowed to by their children. Among many overseas Chinese, idols and photographs of the dead are bowed to, even today.

Nine different words are used in the Old Testament to indicate bowing. They include *avath, cegid, kaphaph, kara, natah, qadad, shachach, shachah,* and *shuwach.* All these words involve the prostrating of oneself to the ground.

Six different words are used in the New Testament to indicate bowing. They are *gonupeteo, kampto, klino, proskuneo, sugkampto,* and *tithemi.* All these words involve kneeling or prostrating oneself to the ground.

A survey of the number of occasions when there were actual bowing ("to bow", "to kneel", "to do obeisance", "to fall at the feet", "to worship", and variant forms of these) in the Bible is shown in the table below.

All the cases of bowing to royalty (i.e. kings, princes and queen) are found only in the Old Testament. Except for five (Rev. 13:4a, 4b, 12; 16:2; 19:20), all the cases of bowing to idols or false gods are found only in the Old Testament. Except for two (Acts 16:29; 10:25), all the cases of bowing to people are also found in the Old Testament. The people bowed to were prominent individuals, including masters, leaders, prophets and officials. Moreover, except for Acts 10:25, the reasons for bowing to these people were clearly not worship. Rather,

Cases of actual bowing	No. of times	Percentage of total
To God/the Lord	98	54%
To angels	9	5%
To royalty	20	11%
To people	26	14%
To Idols/false gods	29	16%
Total	182	100%

Note: References to the same incidents are counted separately, e.g. Acts 9:4; 22:7 and 26:14 are counted as three, not one.

the occasions of bowing were for one or more of these reasons: to honour, to show gratitude, to plead for mercy, to plead for help, or because of fear.

Not all those who knelt before Jesus Christ recognised Him to be divine, at least not before His resurrection. While others knelt to Him in worship, these other people knelt to Him for one or more of the same reasons mentioned above.

In four of the nine cases of bowing to angels (Num. 22:31; Josh. 5:14; Judg. 13:20 and 1 Chron. 21:16), it can be shown that "the angel of the Lord" and "the commander of the Lord's army" were, in fact, the Lord Jesus Christ. The visible manifestations of Jesus Christ to men before His incarnation are called 'theophanies'. Therefore, in these instances, divine worship was rightly given.

We arrive at the following conclusions:

i In the Bible, bowing involves kneeling or prostrating oneself to the ground, and not just stooping the head while standing;

ii A progression from the Old Testament to the New Testament may be noticed, in which bowing becomes increasingly associated with worship (cf. Matt. 4:9; 2:11; Mark 15:19);

iii In the Bible, the number of occasions of bowing to God and the
Lord Jesus Christ is far more than the cases of bowing to creatures;

iv Godly individuals always forbade others to bow down to them
(Esther 3:1-5; Acts 10:25, 26; Rev. 19:9, 10; 22:8, 9);

v From the above points, we conclude that worship is due only to
God, and Christians must not bow (in the sense of kneeling or
prostrating oneself) to any person. If there is any need to show
respect and honour to a person, it is suggested that the Christian
inclines his head, and possibly his upper body, slightly forward,
once.

Appendix 4: CLEAN AND UNCLEAN FOOD

The fourteenth chapter of Romans must not to be confused with the tenth chapter of 1 Corinthians. The former speaks of different types of food, whether they are clean or unclean. The latter speaks of food offered to idols. Jews and Muslims consider pork unclean. Hindus consider the cow sacred and therefore do not take beef. Buddhists consider the killing of living creatures murder and, therefore, do not take meat. Christians consider all food clean (Rom. 14:14, 20).

The apostle Peter once went into a trance and saw the heaven opened and something like a large sheet being let down to earth by its four corners. It contained all kinds of unclean animals, birds and reptiles (Acts 10:9-16). He was commanded by the voice to rise, kill and eat. Three times it happened. Peter learned from this vision the lesson that he was not to call any man impure or unclean (Acts 10:28). This vision would seem to teach also the secondary lesson that Christians must no longer consider the animals, birds and reptiles impure because God has made them clean (Acts 10:15). The Lord Jesus Christ Himself declared all food clean and explained that nothing that enters a man from outside can make him unclean. Rather, it is the evils coming out of man that makes him unclean. These include evil thoughts, sexual-immorality, theft, murder, adultery, greed, malice, deceit, lewdness, envy, slander, arrogance and folly (Mark 7:1-23 cf. 1 Cor. 8:8). "Every creature of God is good, and nothing is to be refused if it is received with thanksgiving, because it is sanctified by the word of God and prayer" (1 Tim. 4:4, 5). "The kingdom of God is not food and drink, but righteousness and peace and joy in the Holy Spirit" (Rom. 14:17).

It may happen that one who was once particular about unclean food is converted and now finds it difficult to take these unclean food. The Bible calls such a person weak. The strong is not to judge the weak, neither is the weak to judge the strong, as far as food and drink are concerned. In all cases, the principle of charity (i.e. love) applies. "All things are lawful for me, but all things are not helpful; all things are lawful for me, but all things do not edify. Let no one seek his own, but each one the other's well-being" (1 Cor. 10:23, 24). If what we eat or drink might cause a weaker brother to stumble, then we are to abstain (Rom. 14:19-21).

Appendix 5: ROMANCE OF THE THREE KINGDOMS

We begin with *Sun Zi's Art of War*. This is probably the oldest book in the world on military strategy. And it is probably the most comprehensive and the most incisive. Written by Sun Wu (Sun Zi's actual name), a contemporary of Confucius, at around 500 BC, the book covers topics such as logistics, terrain, psychology, the use of fire, and the employment of spies. It is not a mere "how-to" book, but one that covers amazingly profound principles in thirteen short chapters. The book has been translated into many languages and are used in many military academies around the world. Napoleon Bonaparte was supposed to have studied a French edition of the book, translated by the French missionary, Amor, in the eighteenth century.

Sun Zi's Art of War is today gaining considerable attention from politicians, economists and businessmen around the world. The principles of war contained in the book are being adapted to business operations, market competition, organisational setups and the deployment of personnel. Some companies in Malaysia are known to have required their employees to attend regular classes on the application of war strategies to business, based on Sun Zi's book.

We turn to another Chinese classic, *The Romance of the Three Kingdoms*, written by Luo Guanzhong round about the year 1368 AD. This book is about the political and military struggles between the three feudal kingdoms of Wei, Shu and Wu in the period 220-265 AD. Many colourful characters feature in this classic, chief of which is Zhuge Liang, also known as Kong Ming, who was the prime minister of the kingdom of Shu. Zhuge Liang applied the military strategies of Sun Zi to great effect. The book consists of many episodes, in which are over forty military clashes. The tactics and battle of wits are interwoven with the behaviour of the various personalities so as to bring out the value of virtues such as loyalty, sincerity, and benevolence.

The average reader will find *Sun Zi's Art of War* a rather dry textbook. He will find *The Romance of the Three Kingdoms* more exciting. He will readily identify with the various characters, with all their ideals, shortcomings, loyalty, treachery, wit, and pettiness. It is no wonder that some politicians in this country are promoting the study of *The Romance of the Three Kingdoms*! It will readily appeal to the ethnic Chinese, and possibly attract many other adherents. The book has been subjected to intensive study – each episode being dissected, analysed, and commented upon. One of the radio channels devoted a session each week to teaching the book. If Sun Zi's book is being treated as a textbook, *The Romance of The Three Kingdoms* is being treated like a holy book.

This is where our concern lies. The Christian who is drawn into such intensive study of the book would have strayed from the path of faith. This is for the following reasons.

Scripture is to be our only authority in all matters of doctrine and practice. It is sufficient for all our needs. It is not a book on science, business, or military strategy, but it contains all the teaching necessary to equip a man to be a godly scientist, a godly businessman, or a godly military officer. Some overzealous and mistaken Christians might want to draw out definite principles of warfare and military tactics from the Bible, just as they have done in the areas of sociology and economics. They believe that there are such things as "Christian banking", "Christian business practice", "Christian astronomy", "Christian sociology", "Christian government", and so on, to which we will not subscribe. We are content with the biblical teaching that "The earth is the Lord's and all its fullness, the world and those who dwell therein" (Ps. 24:1). But that is a digression. We come back to those who are too fascinated with *The Romance of the Three Kingdoms*. To rely on such a book, written by a mere mortal, for guidance in behaviour and life is to deny the sole authority of Scripture.

Then, consider the possible effects of making strategic thinking part-and-parcel of life. Everyone is earning a living in some way, and business dealing is so much an integral part of human relationship. What would become of human relationship if everyone is thinking of others as enemies to conquer and subdue, to gain from and to be taken advantage of? Try to apply the principles of "disrupting the enemy's alliances" to courtship, and "subduing the enemy without fighting" to a business partnership and see what will happen! True, the virtues of loyalty, sincerity and benevolence are encouraged, but the kinds that involve trickery, subterfuge, and the manipulation of people! And what will happen when friends are later perceived of as enemies? No, humanistic teaching should never be made the basis of human relationship, much less the basis of Christian living. We would rather be governed by the teachings of the Bible, and remember that "You shall love the Lord your God with all your heart, with all your soul, and with all your mind," and "You shall love your neighbour as yourself."

The world is already in such a terrible mess – with one nation attacking another, with one ethnic group destroying another, with rampant corruption and oppression in many countries, with criminal activities everywhere causing so much pain and loss. Add to these the natural disasters and accidents that occur everyday. Are there not enough troubles to contend with? There is no need for us to add to the plethora of problems by encouraging greed, selfishness and aggression. Yes, that would be the ultimate effect of encouraging the application of strategic thinking to everyday life – it will actually encourage greed, selfishness and aggression! Qualify it as much as you like. Balance up as much as you like with the call for a caring society. What you will still get is a monster – a smiling, smug, and subtle one!

But wouldn't we be the loser if others apply strategic thinking on us? Shouldn't we know something of how others think and behave? Yes, it will be good to know how others think and behave. No, we will not be the loser if we are the target of strategic thinking. We have our God who will protect us. We have the Holy Spirit who will teach us to "be wise as serpents and harmless as doves". "Do not fear, for those who are with us are more than those who are with them" (2 Kings 6:16). Only trust in the sovereign God, and believe in the sufficiency of the Bible. Read *The Romance of the Three Kingdoms* if you can manage it. It is an exciting book. Study it if you need to. (We are thinking of those who may be students or specialists in the Chinese classics.) But never allow it to replace the Bible.

We have no illusion of the nature of man. He is a sinner bent on evil, godlessness, and self-destruction. The message we will proclaim to the nation, and the world, is, "Repent, and seek peace with God through faith in Jesus Christ!" We have no doubt about the need of the people around us. They are bruised and broken, laden with much care. Our message to them is, "Come to the Lord Jesus Christ, and He will give you rest!"

Appendix 6: CHINA AND THE CHINESE DIASPORA

As China opens up to the world, great interest in this ancient civilisation is aroused everywhere. Businessmen are interested in penetrating this vast market of 1.3 billion people – about a quarter of the world's population! Political observers are anxiously watching to see if this nation, the potential superpower of the new millennium, will be friendly or hostile. This ancient kingdom fascinates historians, anthropologists, linguists and even tourists.

The word 'diaspora' is used in 1 Peter 1:1 in reference to the Christians who were scattered throughout the Roman Empire. The word has been applied to various scattered peoples throughout the world, including the Chinese. I do not claim that my story is typical of overseas Chinese but many who have come to faith in Jesus Christ will be able to identify with it.

Brief history
The Middle Kingdom (for that is what the country is known as in Chinese) has a recorded history of nearly 4000 years. Its oral history goes back much further. The transition into the period of written history occurred during the primitive slave society of the Xia dynasty, which was founded in the 21st century BC. This was followed by the Shang (16th - 11th century BC), the Western Zhou (11th century - 770 BC), and the Eastern Zhou (770 - 221 BC) dynasties. Then came the founding of the Qin dynasty (221-207 BC), when Qin Shi Huangdi united the warring states, standardised the written script, the currencies and the weights and measures, established the system of prefectures and counties and constructed the Great Wall of China.

From the fall of the Qin dynasty in 206 BC to AD 1912, when the People's Republic of China was founded, some fourteen dynasties rose and fell – not bad for a period spanning over 2000 years! The Mongols and the Manchus both conquered and ruled it, but ended up adopting Chinese culture. Trade and diplomatic ties were established along the Silk Routes as well as by sea. Gun powder, paper and printing were invented, the arts flourished, and Chinese culture started to influence neighbouring countries.

The maritime explorations, scientific experiments, and cultural exchanges carried out by Admiral Zheng He (1371-1433/5) in his seven voyages during the Ming dynasty (1368-1644) have attracted attention in recent years (Menzies, 2008, 2009). Groups of Chinese people were left to settle in various parts of the world, intermarrying with the natives of the various countries. Relics and accounts of the Chinese expeditions are still strong in the oral and written traditions of many communities throughout the world. Chinese customs, fishing methods, martial arts, and games were transmitted far and wide. At the height of its international influence, the explorations and interactions with the world were suddenly cut off in 1433. Some claim it was due to the shift of political power from the imperial eunuch party to the scholar-bureaucrats, while others claim that it was due to later implementation of the change of policy of the emperor Zu Di (r. 1402-1424). The superstitious emperor was said to be convinced of heaven's displeasure over the expenses involved in overseas voyages after lightning struck the Forbidden City in 1421, causing a large portion of it to be burnt down. China went into self-imposed seclusion for four hundred years, until the Western powers arrived.

The Middle Kingdom was justifiably proud of its self-sufficiency, until internal decay set in and corruption became pervasive. Britain introduced the opium trade into China, which led to the draining of the economy and disruption of society through the mass addiction of the people. The Opium War of 1840 culminated in the signing of the Treaty of Nanjing with Britain. Enclaves were created along the coast of China in which land was ceded to western nations. The last of these treaties expired in recent years when Hong Kong was returned to China by Britain, and Macau by Portugal.

After the founding of the Republic internal struggles ensued until the Japanese occupation began in 1937. After the withdrawal of the Japanese, the Communist Party, led by Mao Zedong (or Tse-tung) fought with the Kuomintang Party led by Chiang Kaishek. Chiang and his army withdrew to Taiwan, forming a separate island state to which China lays claim to this day.

Civil strife and famine drove many Chinese to seek greener pastures overseas. They were prepared to work hard to eke out a living anywhere – in the gold mines of Australia, the railways of America, the cattle ranches of Argentina, or the tin mines of Malaya. Their frugal living, business acumen and esteem of scholarship meant that subsequent generations became better educated, richer, and more influential. The success of the Chinese is admired – and envied – in many parts of the world.

Today the Han people make up 92% of the population. About 30% are found in the cities and the majority of these would profess to be atheists due to the influence of communism and the effects of the Cultural Revolution. There are over 50 minority groups, including the Buddhists in Tibet, the Muslims in the western provinces, the Christians among the Yi, Miao and Yao tribes of Yunnan, and a number of others. From the perspective of Christian missions, there are about 490 people groups in the country (Hattaway, 2000). Chinese who have emigrated have carried with them the traditional Chinese religion which is a mixture of Confucianism, Taoism and Buddhism. The people of Hong Kong, Macau, Taiwan and Singapore belong to this category.

Conversion of a Chinese pagan
My great grandfather and his son (my grandfather) were among many emigrants to Malaya in the early part of the twentieth century. Both of them died in Malaya.

My father was born in Malaya but was sent back to China when he was six years old, upon the death of his mother. After six years of hard life in China working on the paddy farm, he was sent back to Malaya in the company of an older relative. He worked as a shopkeeper and had six children of whom I am the second. We were told to study and to work hard. We would celebrate the normal festivals, many of which were religious in nature (e.g. the hungry ghost festival), while others were non-religious (e.g. the Chinese New Year). In our home was an altar where the ancestors, idols, and spirits were worshipped.

I would go with my mother to a temple in which were various Chinese deities, including the Goddess of Mercy, and Buddha. She would burn joss-sticks and joss-papers, make offerings and then consult a medium. The medium was a plump man who wore a pair of shorts and no shirt. He would sweat profusely as he went into a trance. The medium would often give out charm papers, on which he has written something with red ink and brush whilst in a trance. To begin a session he would sit by a table and place his head on his hands while invoking the spirit. When the spirit entered him he would begin to mutter and tremble. Suddenly he would hit the table with his hands and jump up to squat on the chair. He would then communicate in an unknown tongue with those who came to see him. While he understood the dialects of the people, he had to make himself understood through an interpreter. The charm papers were kept by the devotees in their wallets or pasted over the door. Sometimes, these were burned and the ashes dropped into a bowl of water to be drunk – for good luck or to cure an illness.

In the mid-1970's I went to England to study, and was invited to a church by Christian friends. The weekly messages soon began to take effect and I was converted. My conversion was a traumatic one in which I shed much tears over my pride and sins. I came into full assurance of salvation immediately and knew God's peace in my heart. Doubts and fears were experienced along the way but, by God's grace, I grew in the grace and knowledge of our Lord. I attempted to learn as much of the Bible as I could before returning to Malaysia.

I discovered very soon that I had to contend with living the Christian life in the Chinese culture. The slick solutions proffered by well-meaning Christians were often inadequate. If everything is to be rejected simply because it is tinged with religion, or is invented by a pagan, or is given a religious sounding name, then the Christian would have to cease to be Chinese! The Bible is our all-sufficient guide. With diligent study, prayer and consultation with friends I learned to separate the cultural from the religious, and to apply the Bible's teaching to the Chinese culture, and avoid compromising Christian truths. There were many stumbles and prayers before I came to a clearer conviction over the many issues. I came to realise that Christians from the same traditional religious background share the same struggles.

We must not make the mistake, however, of thinking that the Chinese need a different gospel, or that the gospel has to be presented to them in a different way. "Faith comes by hearing, and hearing by the word of God" (Romans 10:17). The Chinese, after all, are the descendants of Adam. May many become the children of God!

Recommended Reading

1 Chang, Jung. 1992. Wild Swans: Three Daughters of China. A very readable account of the trauma of three generations in China, caught in the rapid transition from feudalism, through communism, to modernisation.

2 Hattaway, Paul. 2000. Operation China. Piquant.

3 Hsu, C. Y. 1995. The Rise of Modern China, 5th edn. Oxford University Press. A readable history book, covering the culture, politics, and economy of China from 1600 to the present.

4 Kuhn, Isobel. 1983. Nests Above the Abyss. OMF Books. On the evangelisation of the Lisu tribes in Yunnan, south-west China. *Lambert, Tony. 1991. The Resurrection of the Chinese Church. Gives an overview of the revivals and persecution of the church in China.*

5 Li, Zhisui. 1994. The Private Life of Chairman Mao. Random House. A fascinating and somewhat repulsive revelation of this powerful, vain, and lascivious architect of modern China.

6 Menzies, Gavin. 2008. 1421: The Year China Discovered America. HarperCollins Pubs. Inc.

7 Menzies, Gavin: 2009. 1434: The Year A Magnificent Chinese Fleet Sailed To Italy And Ignited The Renaissance. HarperCollins Pubs. Inc.

8 Pan, Lyn. 1993. The Sons of the Yellow Emperor. Mandarin Paperbacks. Contains informative, interesting and heart-rending accounts of the overseas Chinese.

9 Taylor, Dr. and Mrs. Howard. Biography of James Hudson Taylor. 1965. Hodder and Stoughton.

10 Taylor, Mrs. Howard. 1977. Pastor Hsi. OMF Books. On the life and ministry of a converted Confucian scholar and opium addict.

11 Wang, Mingdao. 1981. A Stone Made Smooth. Mayflower Christian Books. Autobiography of a prominent Chinese pastor.

Other books by the same author:

1 A BASIC CATECHISM OF THE CHRISTIAN FAITH

2 A GARDEN ENCLOSED: A Historical Study And Evaluation Of The Form Of Church Government Practised By The Particular Baptists In The 17th And 18th Centuries.

3 AGAINST PARITY: A Response To The Parity View Of The Church Eldership

4 A MULTIFACETED JEWEL: Studies on the Local Church

5 CESSATIONISM OR CONTINUATIONISM?: An Exposition of 1 Corinthians 12-14 and Related Passages

6 FLEE ALSO YOUTHFUL LUSTS: An Exposition of 2 Timothy 2:22

7 GIDEON'S EXPLOITS: Serving God In Challenging Times

8 INDEPENDENCY: The Biblical Form Of Church Government

9 IN SPIRIT AND TRUTH: A Quest For The Biblical Form Of Worship

10 SATAN'S STRATEGY, GOD'S REMEDY (evangelistic booklet)

11 TAMING JACOB: How A Restless Soul Found Peace With God

12 BEWARE OF THE ECUMENICAL AGENDA! A Response to 'More Calvinistic Than Calvin'

13 THE FUNDAMENTALS OF OUR FAITH: Studies On The 1689 Baptist Confession Of Faith

14 THE HIDDEN LIFE: A Call To Discipleship

15 THE KEYS OF THE KINGDOM: A Study On The Biblical Form Of Church Government

16 THE ROSE OF SHARON, THE LILY OF THE VALLEYS: An Exposition on the Song of Solomon

17 THOROUGHGOING REFORMATION: What It Means To Be Truly Reformed

18 WHAT IS A CONFESSIONAL CHURCH?: With The 1689 Confession

19 WHAT IS A REFORMED BAPTIST CHURCH?

20 WORLD MISSIONS TODAY: A Theological, Exegetical, and Practical Perspective Of Missions